Annual Update 2014

US Government & Politics

Anthony J. Bennett

PHILIP ALLAN FOR
HODDER
EDUCATION
AN HACHETTE UK COMPANY

Philip Allan, an imprint of Hodder Education, an Hachette UK company, Market Place, Deddington, Oxfordshire OX15 0SE

Orders

Bookpoint Ltd, 130 Milton Park, Abingdon, Oxfordshire OX14 4SB

tel: 01235 827827

fax: 01235 400401

e-mail: education@bookpoint.co.uk

Lines are open 9.00 a.m.–5.00 p.m., Monday to Saturday, with a 24-hour message answering service. You can also order through www.hoddereducation.co.uk

© Anthony J. Bennett 2014

ISBN 978-1-4718-0471-7

First printed 2014

Impression number 5 4 3 2 1

Year 2016 2015 2014

Typeset by Integra Software Services Pvt. Ltd., Pondicherry, India

Printed by CPI Group (UK) Ltd, Croydon, CR0 4YY

Hachette UK's policy is to use papers that are natural, renewable and recyclable products and made from wood grown in sustainable forests. The logging and manufacturing processes are expected to conform to the environmental regulations of the country of origin.

Contents

Chapter 1

What does Obama's second term cabinet look like?

What you need to know

- The cabinet is the advisory group selected by the president to aid him in making decisions and coordinating the work of the federal government.

- All the heads of the 15 executive departments are automatically members of the cabinet. Others are designated as cabinet members by the president.

- Cabinet members are nominated by the president and must be confirmed by a simple majority in the Senate.

- The president can fire cabinet members as he wishes, while others choose to resign.

- The cabinet meets infrequently and irregularly under most presidents. They mostly function as individuals running their respective departments.

This chapter updates the material in the textbook (Anthony J. Bennett, *A2 US Government and Politics*, 4th edition, 2013) on pages 248–58.

New term: new faces

The most media coverage members of the president's cabinet receive is when they are appointed. After that, most of them might as well have joined the foreign legion: they're never heard from again. Furthermore, far more attention is paid by the media to a president's cabinet at the start of his first term than to the rearrangements that invariably occur at the start of any second term.

President Obama's first term cabinet was noteworthy for its endurance. Presidents Jimmy Carter (1977–81) and George H. W. Bush (1989–93) both lost eight members of their cabinet during their first (in their case, their only) 4 years. Ronald Reagan (1981–85) lost five and Bill Clinton (1993–97) four. But Obama lost only three. Furthermore, one of those — Secretary of Defense Robert Gates — was a holdover from the previous Bush administration. The other two were both from the same post. Obama lost two secretaries of commerce: Gary Locke in 2011 and John Bryson in 2012. Locke was appointed as US ambassador to China; Bryson resigned due to ill health. Thus 13 of Obama's original 15 heads of executive departments served right through the first term, equalling the endurance record set by George W. Bush's first term cabinet. But just as in 2004–05 when Bush began his second term there was something of a mass exodus from the cabinet, the same thing occurred in 2012–13 with eight cabinet posts needing new appointees (see Table 1.1).

Table 1.1 Cabinet changes at the start of Obama's second term

Department	Out	In
State	Hillary Clinton	John Kerry
Treasury	Timothy Geithner	Jacob Lew
Defense	Leon Panetta	Chuck Hagel
Interior	Ken Salazar	Sally Jewell
Commerce	[John Bryson]	Penny Pritzker
Labor	Hilda Solis	Thomas Perez
Transportation	Ray LaHood	Anthony Foxx
Energy	Steven Chu	Ernest Moniz

Some departments experience much more turnover than others. If one traces cabinet appointments over the past 52 years — back to the start of Kennedy's administration in January 1961 — the departments of state, agriculture and interior have had just 15 heads each, averaging around 3½ years in office. But in the same time, the department of commerce, which is already on its third head under this president, has had 23 different cabinet officers averaging only just over 2 years each. The most stable department has been education, with only nine heads since its formation in 1979, and only four in the last 20 years, with no one serving less than 4 years.

Changes at three of the 'big four'

Three of the 'big four' departments — state, treasury and defense — needed new appointees. Only Eric Holder of the 'big four' remained in place into the second term. At the state department it was a case of one big name replacing another. Former first lady, US senator, and defeated candidate in the 2008 Democratic primaries, Hillary Clinton, was replaced by John Kerry, the Democrats' defeated presidential candidate from 2004, and member of the Senate for 28 years. In the previous 20 years only three incumbent members of the Senate had been prepared to give up their seat to serve in the president's cabinet — Lloyd Bentsen of Texas in 1993, and Hillary Clinton of New York and Ken Salazar of Colorado in 2009. It says something about the comparative power and prestige of the Senate and the president's cabinet.

When presidents are looking for potential cabinet recruits, they often look for policy specialists and certainly Obama's recruitment of Kerry to the state department fitted this description. By the time he left the Senate in January 2013 he had just completed 4 years as chairman of the Senate Foreign Relations Committee, a committee he had served on since the 1980s. Kerry is the first white man to head the state department in 16 years — the last four being respectively Madeleine Albright (1997–2001), African Americans Colin Powell (2001–05) and Condoleezza Rice (2005–09), and Hillary Clinton.

Much the same could be said of the appointment of Jacob Lew to be the new secretary of the treasury. 'Jack' Lew spent much of the Clinton administration working in the Office of Management and Budget (OMB) and played a significant role in negotiations leading to the passage of the Balanced Budget Act in 1997. During the Bush years, Lew spent some time working at Citigroup, an international financial services company based in New York. With Obama in the White House, Lew was soon back at OMB where Obama appointed him as director in 2010. In 2012, Obama moved Lew to the pivotal role of White House chief of staff.

Chuck Hagel's appointment to succeed Leon Panetta was the most controversial of these big three appointments. True, Hagel also brought policy specialisation as a former member of the Senate foreign relations and intelligence committees and like John Kerry he is a decorated Vietnam veteran. But unlike Kerry, Clinton and Salazar, Hagel was elected to the Senate as a Republican where he served as a member for Nebraska for 12 years, choosing not to stand for a third term in 2008. But Hagel had been intensely critical of the Bush administration's policies concerning 'the war on terror' and in the Middle East. Thus during his confirmation process in the Senate, Hagel came under friendly fire from his former Republican colleagues rather than from his former Democratic foes.

Senate confirmation

All eight nominees were confirmed by a simple majority of the Senate as required by Article II of the Constitution. But as Table 1.2 shows, some enjoyed more support than others. Some votes were bipartisan; others were marked by high levels of partisanship. The two extremes were Anthony Foxx (Transportation) and Thomas Perez (Labor). Foxx was confirmed by a 100–0 vote. Perez's nomination was filibustered by Republicans and the cloture motion — which required a three-fifths majority — was passed by 60 votes to 40. On this vote six Republicans joined all 54 Democrats to vote 'yes'. But on the substantive motion to confirm Perez, the vote was a strict party line with all 54 Democrats voting 'yes' and all 46 Republicans voting 'no'.

Table 1.2 Senate confirmation votes on Obama cabinet nominees, 2013

Nominee	Position	Senate vote
John Kerry	Secretary of State	94–3
Jacob Lew	Secretary of the Treasury	71–26
Chuck Hagel	Secretary of Defense	58–41
Sally Jewell	Secretary of the Interior	87–11
Penny Pritzker	Secretary of Commerce	97–1
Thomas Perez	Secretary of Labor	54–46
Anthony Foxx	Secretary of Transportation	100–0
Ernest Moniz	Secretary of Energy	97–0

Of the 128 'no' votes across these eight confirmations 126 were cast by Republicans. The remaining two were cast by the independent senator from Vermont Bernie Sanders who voted 'no' on Jacob Lew and Penny Pritzker. Only four Republicans voted 'yes' on Chuck Hagel's nomination.

How quickly did the second term cabinet come together? Well, there are two sides to that question. Once President Obama nominated people, it took an average of just under 60 days for the Democrat-controlled Senate to confirm them (see Table 1.3). This was quicker than the almost 68 days the Republican-controlled Senate took to confirm President Clinton's new cabinet nominees at the start of his second term in 1997. But it was marginally slower than that experienced by the new second term cabinet nominees of presidents Reagan and George W. Bush.

What was slow was the pace at which the President made the nominations. It took Obama nearly 6 months after his re-election to complete his second term cabinet. He did not nominate the new secretary of commerce Penny Pritzker until 2 May 2013. By the time Pritzker took up her new post on 26 June at the department of commerce it was over a year since her predecessor John Bryson had resigned. In the meantime the department had been run by two acting secretaries — Rebecca Blank for just under a year, and then for 3 weeks by Cameron Kerry. Indeed, when Obama held the first cabinet meeting of his second term on 4 March 2013, he had still not nominated new secretaries of labor, transportation or commerce, and the newly nominated secretaries of interior and energy had not yet been confirmed by the Senate.

Table 1.3 Average number of days for Senate to confirm cabinet nominees at start of second term

President	Year	Average time Senate took to confirm initial second term cabinet nominees (days)
Ronald Reagan	1985	56.0
Bill Clinton	1997	67.8
George W. Bush	2005	54.6
Barack Obama	2013	59.8

A balanced cabinet?

Presidents are said to want to appoint a balanced cabinet — in terms of gender, race, age, geographic region and political experience and ideology. So how did Obama do with his second term cabinet?

Gender

Obama's first cabinet contained four female heads of departments — Hillary Clinton (State), Hilda Solis (Labor), Kathleen Sebelius (Health) and Janet

Napolitano (Homeland Security). With Clinton and Solis departing at the end of the first term, Obama was under some pressure to maintain, or possibly increase, the representation of women among the 15 departmental secretaries. Both Clinton and Solis were replaced by men, but two departing men were then replaced by women — Sally Jewell for Ken Salazar at interior, and Penny Pritzker for the long-ago retired John Bryson. So numerically women were at the same number — four out of fifteen — as in 2009. What was different was that now the 'big four' departments — state, treasury, justice and defense — were all headed by men for the first time in 8 years.

Race

Obama's first cabinet had included seven members of minority race. One, Gary Locke at commerce, left early and a further four — Solis (Labor), Salazar (Interior), Chu (Energy) and LaHood (Transportation) — bailed out at the end of the first term. As Locke had not been replaced by a minority appointee, only African-American Eric Holder (Justice) and Japanese-American Eric Shinseki (Veterans' Affairs) were left. Obama's second term cabinet is much less racially balanced than was his first. True, both Lew's and Hagel's parents came from Poland while those of Perez were from the Dominican Republic and Moniz's were Portuguese. Sally Jewell was born in Great Britain. Only African-American Anthony Foxx joined the second term cabinet from what one might call the traditional racial minority groups. In this sense at least, Obama's cabinet look very little like their boss.

Age

Back in 2009, President Obama had appointed a cabinet of whom six were 60 or over. Four of those were gone by the time the second term began — only Sebelius (now 64) and Shinseki (now 70) remained from that group. Three of the new appointees were 60 or over: Hagel (66), Moniz (68) and Kerry (69). At the other end of the scale, Anthony Foxx at 41 became the youngest cabinet appointee under this president, beating Shaun Donovan who had been appointed secretary of housing and urban development aged 42 back in 2009. The average age of the Obama cabinet at the start of the second term was 58, compared with 55 in January 2009.

Geographic region

Presidents like to recruit their cabinet from across the nation rather than from just their own state or region. A president may not have been elected by a majority in every region — the Northeast, the South, the Midwest, or the West — but he needs to make each region feel a part of his administration. Cabinet recruitment is one way he can do this. There is usually a trend, however, that the region — even the state — from which the president comes is well represented. Obama's second term cabinet follows these trends.

Table 1.4 Cabinet members and geographic region, 2013

Region	Cabinet member
West	Eric Shinseki (Hawaii)
	Sally Jewell (Washington)
	Janet Napolitano (Arizona)
Midwest	Chuck Hagel (Nebraska)
	Tom Vilsack (Iowa)
	Kathleen Sebelius (Kansas)
	Penny Pritzker (Illinois)
	Arne Duncan (Illinois)
Northeast	John Kerry (Massachusetts)
	Ernest Moniz (Massachusetts)
	Jacob Lew (New York)
	Thomas Perez (New York and Maryland)
	Shaun Donovan (New York)
	Eric Holder (New York)
South	Anthony Foxx (North Carolina)

Obama's American roots are in the West (Hawaii) and the Midwest (Chicago, Illinois) and eight of the 15 executive department heads come from those two regions, as Table 1.4 shows, including three of the new appointees: Sally Jewell from Washington State, Chuck Hagel from Nebraska, and Penny Pritzker who joins her fellow Chicagoans President Obama and the secretary of education Arne Duncan. But the most well-represented region in Obama's second term cabinet is the North-east with six members including four of the new appointees — Kerry and Moniz from Massachusetts, Perez and Lew from New York, bringing the number of New Yorkers in the cabinet to four. That leaves the new secretary of transportation Anthony Foxx from North Carolina as the only southerner in the cabinet.

One can also see some traditional regional trends in this list. The secretary of the interior Sally Jewell comes from the West; the secretary of agriculture Tom Vilsack from the Midwest; the secretary of the treasury from the Northeast, and so on.

Political experience

As we have already seen, when it comes to cabinet recruitment the president is usually looking for policy specialists — and this is true for a large number of Obama's cabinet members. We saw this in the professional backgrounds of John Kerry, Chuck Hagel and Jack Lew. The new secretary of energy Ernest Moniz was until early 2013 Director of the Laboratory for Energy and the Environment at the Massachusetts Institute of Technology; the new secretary of commerce Penny Pritzker is a business executive and entrepreneur — and the world's 651st richest person.

Table 1.5 Cabinet members with previous elective experience (new members in bold)

Cabinet member	Previous elective office	State/city
Tom Vilsack	Governor	Iowa
Kathleen Sebelius	Governor	Kansas
Janet Napolitano	Governor	Arizona
John Kerry	Senator	Massachusetts
Chuck Hagel	Senator	Nebraska
Anthony Foxx	Mayor	Charlotte, North Carolina

But presidents will also want some political experience in the cabinet. After all, cabinet officers live and work in the political world; they have to deal with politicians. Obama's second term cabinet contains three former governors, two former senators and one former city mayor (see Table 1.5). Having had eight consecutive secretaries of state who had no experience of elective politics — from Alexander Haig in 1981 to Condoleezza Rice through to 2009 — we have now had two secretaries of state both of whom were recruited from the Senate, and both of whom had been involved in presidential campaigns, Kerry in 2004 and Clinton in 2008. Anthony Foxx is the first former city mayor to serve in the cabinet since Henry Cisneros, the former mayor of San Antonio, Texas, served as secretary of housing in Bill Clinton's first term. But again, notice the link with policy — city mayors and housing.

Political ideology

Another trend in appointing the cabinet is to have a mix of political ideology — conservatives and liberals — as well as sometimes a person from the opposite party. Barack Obama's first term cabinet included Ray LaHood who for 14 years (1995–2009) was a Republican member of the House of Representatives from Illinois. Sixty-seven-year-old LaHood stepped down at the start of the second term. But, as we have already seen, Obama included another former Republican member of Congress in his new team — former Republican senator from Nebraska, Chuck Hagel. In an era of such partisan politics in Washington DC it is perhaps surprising that this particular tradition still survives.

Cabinet meetings

President Obama held just 16 cabinet meetings during his first term: five in 2009, four in each of 2010 and 2011, and just three in 2012, one of which was after Obama's re-election. The record for the second term appears even more patchy. When the cabinet met for its first meeting of the new administration on 4 March 2013, this was only the third cabinet meeting in over a year. And, as we have already seen, it was a somewhat patchy membership that attended, with many new positions still incomplete.

At the start of this meeting, the President welcomed Jack Lew and Chuck Hagel, both of whom had already been confirmed in their new positions. Interestingly, the new secretary of state John Kerry was absent — represented by the department's under secretary for political affairs Wendy Sherman. This raises an interesting question concerning attendance. In an interview in 1981 in his office at the top of the then World Trade Center in New York, President Nixon's former secretary of commerce Peter Peterson told me that 'you certainly did not send your number two along because you were too busy or didn't want to go'. President Ford's former secretary of transportation William Coleman told me that 'if I had another engagement, I would cancel it, unless it was *very* important'. Other former cabinet members told me, however, that things often clashed with cabinet meetings as the latter were often scheduled irregularly and with little warning. It was almost as if the president thought, 'Oh, we haven't had a cabinet meeting for some time — we'd better call one!' On 4 March 2013, the media reported that John Kerry was in the United Arab Emirates (UAE) at a meeting of the US–UAE Business Council. The UAE was the eighth country Kerry had visited on what was his first overseas trip. Clearly this was a good reason to send his number two to the cabinet meeting.

In that March 2013 meeting, the President laid out his agenda in the brief media photo opportunity that Obama permits just before the formal part of the meeting begins. The meeting's agenda included the effects of the recent budget sequestration, comprehensive immigration reform, and the vice-president and others reporting on proposals to reduce gun violence in America.

It was reported in the American media later in the year that the President and the first lady had invited all the cabinet for an 'all-day retreat' on Friday 26 July at Camp David, the presidential retreat 60 miles northwest of Washington DC. This was a brave move, for the history of Camp David cabinet get-togethers is not promising. When President Carter tried one in 1979, the result was a slanging match between senior White House aides and cabinet members with the President cast in the uncomfortable role of referee. President Clinton tried one in 1993 which the then secretary of labor Robert Reich remembers with a mixture of tongue-in-cheek humour and horror in his political biography *Locked in the Cabinet* (see Box 1.1). One trusts that Obama's Camp David get-together was rather more profitable.

What role for the cabinet?

In answering this question, one needs to be careful. Are we talking about the cabinet as a collectivity — when it meets together with the president — or are we talking about the cabinet as individuals? 'Obama's second term cabinet to play bigger policy role', headlined an article in the *Washington Post* 2 months into Obama's second term. Did this mean more cabinet meetings where important policy decisions would be made? Probably not. What the article was suggesting was that individual cabinet officers in certain policy areas might take on a higher level of importance in policy development and enactment. Examples given included Ernest Moniz, the new secretary of energy, and climate change.

30 January 1993, Camp David, Maryland

FDR called this place 'Shangri-la,' but nothing about it conjures up exotic adventure. It's a set of mildewed cabins in the woods. The whole cabinet is here, along with Bill and Hillary. We came by bus — the cabinet packed together like furniture in a U-Haul truck. The purpose of the conclave isn't entirely clear. We make a long list of what we want to accomplish over the next four years. Making long lists in the woods is exhilarating. Figuring out exactly how to do even a small part of this agenda is presumably less so. After dinner we gather around the fire. A hard day of list-making creates a degree of camaraderie. Now comes the forced intimacy. The 'facilitator' asks us each to tell something about ourselves that the others are unlikely to know. Self-disparaging stories tumble out, awkwardly at first. Bill talks of being mocked as a fat kid at school.

Extract from Robert Reich, *Locked in the Cabinet,* Alfred Knopf, 1997

One thing Obama does need to do during his second term is to improve the relations between his White House staff and the cabinet. Historically this has always been a problematic relationship: White House staffers see cabinet members as disloyal; cabinet members see White House staffers as egotistical control freaks. In his March 2013 article, Philip Rucker stated:

> Relations between the White House and the Cabinet were badly frayed during Obama's first term when agency chiefs complained that White House officials micromanaged their departments and were unwilling to accept their policy input. The White House embraced a few cabinet superstars such as Education Secretary Arne Duncan, an Obama friend, but others complained that they were not made to feel as if they were part of the team.

But presidential scholar Stephen Hess was sceptical. According to Hess, empowering his cabinet members during his second term 'would be a reversal of form for this president in particular, but for recent presidents as well'. He continued:

> It's easy to make promises. You didn't appoint somebody and say, 'Hey, I'm putting you in this office but I'm not really going to give you much to do.'

One former cabinet member told me that when Richard Nixon appointed him, the president remarked 'Look, you can either "do things" or "be someone".' This cabinet member went on to say:

> What Nixon meant by that was that in his administration the people who 'did things' were those in the White House. It was they who would really give the president any advice he sought. But if you wanted to 'be someone' — you know, have the big limousine and so on — then you became a cabinet officer. A cabinet member's job was not one of great power or influence in government.

Not much has changed in the last 40 years.

Questions

1 How many of Obama's original cabinet served throughout his first term?
2 Which departments are (a) the least stable, and (b) the most stable in terms of departmental heads?
3 Give brief biographies of (a) John Kerry, (b) Jacob Lew and (c) Chuck Hagel.
4 What does Table 1.2 tell us about the Senate's confirmation of Obama's new cabinet members?
5 Is Obama's second term cabinet more or less balanced than his first term cabinet with regard to (a) gender and (b) race?
6 Give two other examples of 'balance' in Obama's new cabinet.
7 Give three examples of policy specialists in Obama's new cabinet.
8 Give three examples of former elective politicians in Obama's new cabinet.
9 How often does Obama meet with his cabinet?
10 Comment on the relationship between Obama's cabinet and his White House staff. How does this compare with previous administrations?

Chapter 2

'President Romney': another near-miss Electoral College oddity

What you need to know

- The Electoral College is the institution established by the Founding Fathers to indirectly elect the president.
- Each state has a certain number of votes in the Electoral College equal to the state's representation in Congress (i.e. House plus Senate).
- There are 538 Electoral College votes altogether.
- To win the presidency, a candidate needs to win an absolute majority of Electoral College votes, i.e. 270.
- All but two of the states (Maine and Nebraska) automatically award all their Electoral College votes to the candidate who wins the most popular votes in their state — the 'winner takes all' system.

This chapter updates the material in the textbook (Anthony J. Bennett, *A2 US Government and Politics*, 4th edition, 2013) on pages 92–98.

The lesson of 2000

Doubtless you will be familiar with the exceedingly odd result produced by the Electoral College in the 2000 presidential election. On Election Day in November, Democrat Al Gore won 51 million votes and Republican George W. Bush just over 50.4 million votes. But when it came to the voting of the Electoral College in mid-December, Bush won 271 electoral votes to Gore's 266. The Electoral College had elected the popular vote loser for the first time since 1888.

This Electoral College oddity caused much discontent, especially among Democrats. It also led to much discussion among politicians and academics as to how to reform the Electoral College to make such results even less likely, or impossible. At that time, many politicians and academics pointed out the seeming advantages of the way in which Maine and Nebraska awarded their Electoral College votes — in a more proportional way. Rather than using the 'winner takes all' system adopted by the other 48 states and the District of Columbia, in which the winner of the statewide popular vote wins all that state's electoral votes, Maine and Nebraska award their electoral votes by congressional district.

The benefits of proportionality

The seeming benefit of this system was shown in 2008 when Nebraska's five electoral votes were divided between John McCain and Barack Obama. Nebraska has three congressional districts — one for each of its House members — plus, of course, two senators and therefore five electoral votes. As Table 2.1 shows, John McCain comfortably won the first and third districts but Barack Obama just won the second district — centred on the city of Omaha. McCain won the state overall. This resulted in four electoral votes going to McCain — one for each district he won, plus two for winning the statewide vote — with one vote going to Obama. The virtues of this apparently fairer system were extolled by would-be reformers, and during the last decade or so, a number of other states have seriously considered adopting it.

Table 2.1 Awarding of electoral votes in Nebraska, 2008

	McCain (%)	Obama (%)	Electoral votes
First District	54.10	44.33	McCain 1
Second District	48.75	49.97	Obama 1
Third District	68.64	29.63	McCain 1
Statewide	56.53	41.60	McCain 2
Total:			McCain 4/Obama 1

In the four presidential elections held between 1984 and 1996, the congressional district system would have given a more fair and accurate representation of the popular vote than did the winner-takes-all system, as Table 2.2 shows. So, for example, in 1996 Clinton and Dole (who split the popular vote 49%–40%) would have split the electoral votes 64%–36% rather than 70%–30%.

Table 2.2 Winner-takes-all and district systems compared: 1984–96

Year	Candidates	Popular vote (%)	ECV (%) Winner takes all	ECV (%) District system
1984	Reagan	58.8	97.6	87.7
	Mondale	40.6	2.4	12.3
1988	Bush	53.4	79.2	68.6
	Dukakis	45.7	20.8	31.4
1992	Clinton	43.0	68.8	60.0
	Bush	37.5	31.2	40.0
	Perot	18.9	0.0	0.0
1996	Clinton	49.2	70.4	64.1
	Dole	40.7	29.6	35.9

Some drawbacks too

But in the next four elections — 2000–12 — the congressional district system would actually have produced more problematic results than the winner-takes-all system in three of those four elections, all bar 2008.

In 2000, the congressional district would actually have made things worse by giving popular vote loser George W. Bush an even more lopsided victory in the Electoral College. Instead of giving Bush 271 electoral votes, under the district system Bush would have won 288 electoral votes with just 250 for Gore, making a bad result even worse. In 2004, Bush won 50.7% of the popular vote and 53.1% of the Electoral College votes. But under the congressional district system, Bush would have won 317 rather than 286 electoral votes — just under 59% (see Table 2.3).

However, in the 2008 election, the congressional district would have worked well. Obama, who won 53% of the popular vote, would have had 56% of the Electoral College votes, with McCain winning 46% of the popular vote and 44% of the Electoral College vote — an almost perfect fit, and certainly much fairer than the 68%–32% split which the winner-takes-all system gave.

Table 2.3 Winner-takes-all and district systems compared: 2000–08

Year	Candidates	Popular vote (%)	ECV (%) Winner takes all	ECV (%) District system
2000	Bush	47.9	50.4	53.5
	Gore	48.4	49.6	46.5
2004	Bush	50.7	53.1	58.9
	Kerry	48.3	46.9	40.1
2008	Obama	52.9	67.8	55.9
	McCain	45.7	32.2	44.1

So, of the seven elections held between 1984 and 2008, the district system would have given a better result in five elections with the winner-takes-all system performing better only twice. But what would have happened in 2012 had all 50 states and the District of Columbia used the congressional district system?

Proportionality and 2012

Table 2.4 gives us the data and the answer. Column 2 shows that of the 435 congressional districts, President Obama won 209 of them plus the District of Columbia, which for the purpose of this exercise counts as one, giving him a total at the bottom of column 2 of 210. Column 3 shows Mitt Romney winning the remaining 226 congressional districts — 17 more than the President. This is the first surprising piece of evidence that although Obama won 5 million more votes than Romney, Romney won the popular vote in more districts than Obama.

Table 2.4 also shows us the states in which it was most significant that although Obama won the popular vote statewide, Romney won in a majority of districts. There were six states in which this occurred: Florida, Michigan, Ohio, Pennsylvania, Virginia and Wisconsin. These states commanded a total of 106 Electoral College votes — more than one-third of the 270 required to win the White House. Because all six states used the winner-takes-all system, all these 106 electoral votes went to Obama. Romney scored zero. But under the congressional district system Obama would have won only 44 of them with Romney winning 62.

Table 2.4 2012 election by congressional districts and states

State	Obama Districts	Romney Districts	Statewide winner	Total Obama	Total Romney
Alabama	1	6	Romney	1	8
Arizona	3	6	Romney	3	8
Arkansas	0	4	Romney	0	6
California	41	12	Obama	43	12
Colorado	4	3	Obama	6	3
Connecticut	5	0	Obama	7	0
Delaware	1	0	Obama	3	0
District of Columbia	1	0	Obama	3	0
Florida	11	16	Obama	13	16
Georgia	4	10	Romney	4	12
Hawaii	2	0	Obama	4	0
Idaho	0	2	Romney	0	4
Illinois	12	6	Obama	14	6
Indiana	2	7	Romney	2	9
Iowa	3	1	Obama	5	1
Kansas	0	4	Romney	0	6
Kentucky	1	5	Romney	1	7
Louisiana	1	5	Romney	1	7
Maine	2	0	Obama	4	0
Maryland	7	1	Obama	9	1
Massachusetts	9	0	Obama	11	0
Michigan	5	9	Obama	7	9
Minnesota	6	2	Obama	8	2
Mississippi	1	3	Romney	1	5
Missouri	2	6	Romney	2	8
Montana	0	1	Romney	0	3
Nebraska	0	3	Romney	0	5

State	Obama Districts	Romney Districts	Statewide winner	Total Obama	Total Romney
Nevada	3	1	Obama	5	1
New Hampshire	2	0	Obama	4	0
New Jersey	8	4	Obama	10	4
New Mexico	2	1	Obama	4	1
New York	24	3	Obama	26	3
North Carolina	3	10	Romney	3	12
North Dakota	0	1	Romney	0	3
Ohio	4	12	Obama	6	12
Oklahoma	0	5	Romney	0	7
Oregon	4	1	Obama	6	1
Pennsylvania	5	13	Obama	7	13
Rhode Island	2	0	Obama	4	0
South Carolina	1	6	Romney	1	8
South Dakota	0	1	Romney	0	3
Tennessee	2	7	Romney	2	9
Texas	11	25	Romney	11	27
Utah	0	4	Romney	0	6
Vermont	1	0	Obama	3	0
Virginia	4	7	Obama	6	7
Washington	7	3	Obama	9	2
West Virginia	0	3	Romney	0	5
Wisconsin	3	5	Obama	5	5
Wyoming	0	1	Romney	0	3
Totals	**210**	**226**	Obama **27** Romney **24**	**264**	**274**

The most stunning result would have been in Ohio where although Obama won statewide, Romney won in 12 of the state's 16 congressional districts. But whereas Romney won most of his districts quite narrowly — seven of them by a margin of less than 10 percentage points — Obama won his four by huge margins. He won the 13th District by over 27 percentage points, the 9th District centred on the city of Toledo by over 36 points, the 3rd District, including Columbus and Dayton, by over 40 points, and the 11th District — the City of Cleveland — by over 66 points, winning 83% of the popular vote to Romney's 16%. It is these quirks which caused the distortion.

The fourth column in Table 2.4 shows that Obama won the statewide vote in 26 states plus Washington DC, with Romney the winner in the remaining 24. That would give Obama an additional 54 Electoral College votes and Romney an

additional 48. Adding Obama's 210 in column 2 to his 54 (27 x 2) from column 4 gives him a total of 264 in column 5. Adding Romney's 226 in column 3 to his 48 (24 x 2) from column 4 gives him a total of 274 in column 6.

So, had the 2012 election been run on the congressional district system, 20 January 2013 would have seen Chief Justice John Roberts begin the administration of the oath of office to the forty-fifth president of the United States: 'I Willard Mitt Romney do solemnly swear', and the Democrats would have claimed to have been cheated out of the White House in two elections out of four. Who then would have been writing the obituary of the Republican Party? Maybe Romney didn't do that badly after all.

Questions

1 What was odd about the 2000 presidential election result?
2 How do Maine and Nebraska differ from the other 48 states in the way they award their Electoral College votes? Explain what is meant by the 'district system'.
3 What happened in Nebraska in the 2008 election?
4 Analyse the data presented in Table 2.2. Which system would have produced the fairer results?
5 What does Table 2.3 show about the effect the district system would have had on the 2000, 2004 and 2008 elections?
6 Explain the data presented in Table 2.4. What is especially noteworthy about the data for Florida, Michigan, Ohio, Pennsylvania, Virginia and Wisconsin?
7 Which do you think is the better system? Explain your answer.

Chapter 3

Race, rights and the Supreme Court

What you need to know

- The Supreme Court is the highest federal court in the USA.
- The Court is made up of nine justices, appointed by the president, for life.
- Of the current nine justices, five were appointed by Republican presidents and four by Democrats.
- The Supreme Court has the power of judicial review. This is the power to declare acts of Congress or actions of the executive branch — or acts or actions of state governments — unconstitutional, and thereby null and void.
- By this power of judicial review, the Court acts as the umpire of the Constitution and plays a leading role in safeguarding Americans' rights and liberties.
- Affirmative action is a programme that entails giving those members of a previously disadvantaged minority group a headstart in such areas as higher education and employment.

This chapter updates the material in the textbook (Anthony J. Bennett, *A2 US Government and Politics*, 4th edition, 2013) on the Supreme Court on pages 314–27, on Affirmative Action on pages 348–57, and on Propositions on pages 109–11.

The previous Supreme Court term (2011–12) had given us the blockbuster decision on the constitutional standing of President Obama's healthcare reform legislation. It was a hard act to follow. But the 2012–13 term was no damp squib, with four highly significant rulings — one on affirmative action, one on the 1965 Voting Rights Act, and two on the issue of same-sex marriage.

Table 3.1 Significant Supreme Court decisions, 2012–13 term

Case	Concerning	Decision
Fisher v *University of Texas*	A race-conscious admissions programme at the University of Texas	7–1
Shelby County v *Holder*	Part of the 1965 Voting Rights Act that subjected states with a history of discrimination to federal oversight	5–4
United States v *Windsor*	The 1996 Defense of Marriage Act which denied federal benefits to married same-sex couples	5–4
Hollingsworth v *Perry*	California's Proposition 8 (2008) defining marriage as being only between a man and woman	5–4

What did the Court do about affirmative action?

The decision in *Fisher* v *University of Texas* was maybe the most anticipated of the Court's term as it was the Court's first major ruling on affirmative action since its landmark decision in 2003 in *Grutter* v *Bollinger*. That had been a 5–4 decision with the majority opinion written by Justice Sandra Day O'Connor. But O'Connor had since retired, as had two of the justices who had joined her in that decision — John Paul Stevens and David Souter. Furthermore, O'Connor had been replaced by the more reliably conservative justice Samuel Alito. So all eyes were on the Court to see whether the Court would still regard race-conscious admissions programmes in schools and places of higher education as constitutional. Put simply: was affirmative action still allowed, or did the majority of the Court now regard it as past its sell-by date?

The case was brought by Abigail Fisher, a young woman from Texas, who applied to the University of Texas at Austin but was rejected. Fisher, who was white, then filed a lawsuit arguing that she had been the victim of racial discrimination because minority race students with less impressive qualifications than hers had been accepted. The university had won the case in the lower federal courts but found a more sceptical audience at the Supreme Court. In a 7–1 decision — Justice Kagan did not participate, having already worked on the case as Solicitor General before being appointed to the Court — the Court ruled that the university's use of race in its admissions policy must meet a test known as 'strict scrutiny'. In his majority opinion, Justice Anthony Kennedy stated that in their rulings, the lower courts had failed to apply such strict scrutiny.

The majority decision declared the lower appeal court decision void and instructed that court to rehear the case using the stricter criteria. The lone dissenter was Justice Ruth Bader Ginsburg who wanted to uphold the decision of the lower court. In her view, the University of Texas considers race in admissions only as 'a factor of a factor of a factor of a factor'.

What does this strict scrutiny involve? Justice Kennedy made that clear in his opinion. 'Strict scrutiny imposes on the university the ultimate burden of demonstrating, before turning to racial classifications, that available, workable, race-neutral alternatives do not suffice.' Kennedy added that 'the reviewing court must ultimately be satisfied that no workable race-neutral alternatives would produce the educational benefits of diversity.' As a result, courts will no longer be able to simply rubber-stamp a university's claim that it needs affirmative action in order to produce a racially diverse student body.

The supporters of affirmative action had feared the worst: that the Supreme Court would declare the use of race-conscious admissions programmes to be unconstitutional. Given that the justices had taken 9 months from oral argument to decide the case, the 7–1 margin was something of a surprise. It is likely, therefore, that the decision they eventually announced was a compromise cobbled together from a number of conflicting opinions, none of which could command a majority. Supporters of affirmative action were therefore a little relieved. At least their arguments live to fight another day (see Box 3.1).

One likely consequence of this decision is that numerous other race-conscious admissions programmes will now be challenged in the federal courts, and when that happens they will face the safe 'strict scrutiny' that the University of Texas programme will face when it returns to court in the coming months. In the end, this was the 'dog that didn't bark' kind of story, but it was a decision which according to the *New York Times*' Adam Liptak was 'simultaneously modest and significant'.

Box 3.1 **Reaction to *Fisher* v *University of Texas***

- 'We remain committed to assembling a student body that provides the educational benefits of diversity while respecting the rights of all students and acting within the constitutional framework established by the Court.' (William C. Powers, President, University of Texas)
- 'The Supreme Court has established such exceptionally high hurdles that it is unlikely that most institutions will be able to overcome them.' (Edward Blum, conservative lawyer who instigated the appeal to the Supreme Court)
- 'The Supreme Court has again upheld the principles behind race-conscious affirmative action but it has, wittingly or not, continued its drift away from the ideals it advanced in the civil rights era beginning with *Brown* v *Board of Education*.' (Lee Bollinger, law professor who was the named defendant in the 2003 affirmative action case)
- 'I am grateful to the justices for moving the nation closer to the day when a student's race isn't used at all in college admissions.' (Abigail Fisher, who brought the case claiming racial discrimination)
- 'For supporters of affirmative action, I'd put this decision in the category of "disaster averted" rather than "victory achieved".' (David Strauss, University of Chicago law professor)

Key part of the Voting Rights Act invalidated

The Court handed down a second important decision concerning race in *Shelby County* v *Holder*. At issue were some provisions of a now 48-year-old law — the 1965 Voting Rights Act — and specifically whether these provisions were any longer properly applicable in the second decade of the twenty-first century. In 1982, Congress renewed the Act for a further 25 years. One year before its expiration in 2007, Congress passed and President George W. Bush signed into law a further 25-year extension of the Act. The law applied to nine states (see Box 3.2) and to scores of counties and municipalities in other states such as the Bronx, Manhattan and Brooklyn in New York. The law was aimed at correcting decades of historic racial discrimination in voting rights. The Act established extensive federal government oversight of voting laws and practices in these states and jurisdictions.

Box 3.2	States to which the provisions of the 1965 Voting Rights Act applied

Alabama	Georgia	South Carolina
Alaska	Louisiana	Texas
Arizona	Mississippi	Virginia

In order to understand this 2013 decision we need to understand two specific parts of the 1965 Voting Rights Act. **Section 5** requires certain states and jurisdictions to obtain prior permission — 'preclearance' — from either the Attorney General of the United States or a three judge federal court panel that any changes they are proposing in their voting laws or practices do not 'deny or abridge the right to vote on account of race, color, or membership in a language minority group'. **Section 4(b)** of the Act contains a formula that determines which states and jurisdictions are subject to this federal government preclearance.

Section 5 was initially set to expire after just 5 years but subsequent amendments to the Act extended Section 5's life, and in 1972 the Section 4(b) formula was updated. But in 2006 when Section 5 was extended for another 25 years it relied on the 1972 formula to decide which states and localities were covered by the Act. At issue, therefore, in this case was whether this decades-old formula was still appropriate and constitutionally defendable. In a 5–4 decision, the Court ruled that it was not. It therefore found that in reauthorising Section 5 of the Voting Rights Act under the pre-existing formula, Congress exceeded its authority under the Fourteenth and Fifteenth Amendments.

Unlike the previous case, in which a judicious compromise had been worked out, this decision split the Court along ideological lines with the conservative quartet (see Table 3.2) joined by Justice Anthony Kennedy forming the five-member majority. By comparing the majority opinion — authored by Chief Justice John Roberts — and the minority dissent — authored by Justice Ruth Bader Ginsburg — one can see that the two sides drew sharply different lessons from the history of the civil rights movement and the nation's progress in rooting out racial discrimination in voting. In the view of Adam Liptak ('Supreme Court invalidates key part of Voting Rights Act', *New York Times*, 25 June 2013) 'at the core of the disagreement was whether racial minorities continued to face barriers to voting in states with a history of racial discrimination'.

Table 3.2 The ideological line-up of the Supreme Court, 2012–13

Liberal quartet	Swing justice	Conservative quartet
Ruth Bader Ginsburg	Anthony Kennedy	John Roberts
Stephen Breyer		Antonin Scalia
Sonia Sotomayor		Clarence Thomas
Elena Kagan		Samuel Alito

Chief Justice Roberts for the majority believed that 'our country has changed'. He recalled the Freedom Summer of 1964. He mentioned Bloody Sunday in 1965 when police officers beat the black marchers in Selma, Alabama. Roberts drew attention to the fact that today this town is governed by an African-American mayor. In the majority's view 'whilst any racial discrimination in voting is too much, Congress must ensure that the legislation it passes to remedy that problem speaks to current conditions'. According to the majority, Congress could try to impose oversight on states and local jurisdictions where they believed voting rights were at risk, but they must do so based on up-to-date data and an up-to-date formula.

According to Roberts, the trouble at present is that the current system is 'based on 40-year-old facts having no logical relationship to the present day'. He continued 'Congress — if it is to divide the states — must identify those jurisdictions to be singled out on a basis that makes sense in the light of current conditions. It cannot simply rely on the past.' What the Court did, therefore, was to leave Section 5 of the Act still standing, but by declaring Section 4(b) unconstitutional Section 5 becomes inoperable. Put simply — no formula, no oversight. It remains a moot point as to whether the Court as currently constituted might not also in some future case declare Section 5 unconstitutional as well. In a concurring opinion, Justice Clarence Thomas declared that this was his opinion, stating that in his view the Court had merely left 'the inevitable conclusion unstated.' Critics of Section 5 say that it is an unconstitutional infringement of states' rights under the Tenth Amendment.

> ### Box 3.3 Justice Ruth Bader Ginsburg on *Shelby County* v *Holder*
>
> Beyond question, the Voting Rights Act is no ordinary legislation. It is extraordinary because Congress embarked on a mission long delayed and of extraordinary importance: to realise the purpose and promise of the Fifteenth Amendment. For half a century a concerted effort has been made to end racial discrimination in voting. Thanks to the Voting Rights Act, progress once the subject of a dream has been achieved and continues to be made. The Court errs egregiously by overriding Congress's decision.

In her dissent (see Box 3.3), Justice Ginsburg — joined by justices Stephen Breyer, Sonia Sotomayor and Elena Kagan — cited the words of the Reverend Dr Martin Luther King Jr and said his legacy and the nation's commitment to justice had been 'disserved by today's decision'. She said the law had properly changed from 'first-generation barriers to ballot access' such as poll tax and literacy tests to 'second-generation barriers' such as racial gerrymandering. Roberts had drawn one lesson from Selma, Alabama, but Ginsburg drew another. Referring to Dr King she wrote: 'The great man who led the march from Selma to Montgomery and there called for the passage of the Voting Rights Act foresaw progress, even in Alabama.' It was her belief that Congress was the right body to decide whether the

law was still needed and where. Congress reauthorised the Act in 2006 by large majorities: 390–33 in the House; 98–0 in the Senate. A Republican president had signed the reauthorised Act into law — what Ginsburg saw as 'an example of our continued commitment to a united America where every person is valued and treated with dignity and respect'.

The decision will have immediate consequences. Within days of the decision Texas announced that a voter identification law that had been blocked would go into immediate effect and that the state's redistricting maps would no longer need federal government approval. True, Congress was told that it could draw up new criteria for Section 4(b) but in the current partisan atmosphere that will be far from easy and certainly not quick. President Obama, whose election is often cited by those who say the Act is no longer needed, said he was 'deeply disappointed' by the Court's decision.

Court boosts same-sex marriage rights

The Court issued two decisions which boosted the movement towards the acceptance of same-sex marriage. In *United States* v *Windsor* the Court declared the 1996 Defense of Marriage Act (DOMA) unconstitutional principally because it resulted in the 'deprivation of the liberty of the person protected by [the Due Process clause of] the Fifth Amendment'. Justice Anthony Kennedy wrote the majority opinion joined by the Court's liberal quartet (see Table 3.2). Justice Antonin Scalia wrote the dissenting opinion on behalf of the Court's conservative quartet. The essence of the Court's ruling was that by defining marriage as a union only between a man and a woman, same-sex couples who were legally married in states that recognised such unions were denied federal government benefits due to married couples.

First, a quick bit of background. In 1996, the DOMA was passed by overwhelming majorities in both houses of Congress: by 85–14 in the Senate; by 342–67 in the House. President Clinton was not then in favour of same-sex marriage but he disliked the legislation. However, as it had passed both houses with veto-proof majorities, Clinton decided to sign it into law in order to avoid the kind of political damage he had suffered 3 years earlier with his attempt to allow gays to serve openly in the US military. Eleven years later, Edith Windsor and Thea Spyer, two women residents of New York, were lawfully married as a same-sex couple in Ontario, Canada. Two years later Spyer died leaving her entire estate to Windsor. Windsor sought to claim the federal estate tax exemption for surviving spouses but was barred from doing so by Section 3 of the DOMA (see Box 3.4). The Internal Revenue Service said that the tax exemption did not apply to same-sex marriages and billed her for $363,053 in estate taxes. When the case came to court, the US Attorney General Eric Holder issued a statement on behalf of the Obama administration saying that he agreed with Windsor's position, that in his view the 1996 Act was unconstitutional, and he would no longer defend the law in court.

The decision is of double significance for not only did the majority strike down the Defense of Marriage Act — a federal law — but the same arguments could well be made in legal challenges to state bans on same-sex marriage, a point not lost on the dissenting foursome. 'The federal statute is invalid,' wrote Justice Kennedy for the majority, 'for no legitimate purpose overcomes the purpose and effect to disparage and injure those whom the state, by its marriage laws, sought to protect in personhood and dignity.' Justice Kennedy continued: 'By seeking to displace this protection and treating those persons as living in marriages less respected than others, the federal statute is in violation of the Fifth Amendment.' Kennedy added that the ruling applied only to marriages from states that allowed same-sex couples to wed.

For the dissenting minority, Justice Scalia called the latter declaration 'real cheek'. 'By formally declaring anyone opposed to same-sex marriage an enemy of human decency, the majority arms well every challenger to a state law restricting marriage to its traditional definition,' declared Scalia.

The case of *Hollingsworth* v *Perry* was decided on a technicality — but again by a 5–4 division of the Court. California's ban on same-sex marriage had been enacted by a ballot initiative known as Proposition 8 in 2008 (see Box 3.5). It was passed by 52% to 48%. In May 2009, Kristin Perry and Sandra Stier were denied a marriage licence because they were a same-sex couple. Perry went to the federal courts alleging that the law was unconstitutional because it violated the Due Process and Equal Protection clauses of the Fourteenth Amendment. The federal trial court found for the plaintiff and ruled the law unconstitutional. The State of California declined to appeal the decision but the proponents of Proposition 8 were permitted to do so in their place. But it was the appearance of these supporters of Proposition 8 as plaintiffs in the appeal before the Supreme Court which caused the 'technical' problem. For five of the justices declined to revisit the lower federal courts' decision because in their view the Proposition 8 proponents had suffered only 'generalised grievance' and therefore lacked 'appellate standing' before the Court. They were not therefore entitled to represent the state's interest in the case. The Supreme Court decision sent the case back to the federal appeals court in San Francisco 'with instructions to dismiss the appeal for lack of jurisdiction'. That meant that the trial court's decision to declare the law unconstitutional was left standing.

Box 3.5 California's Proposition 8 (2008)

Section 1: This measure shall be known and may be cited as the 'California Marriage Protection Act'.

Section 2: Article I Section 7.5 is added to the California Constitution, to read: Only marriage between a man and a woman is valid or recognized in California.

But this 5–4 division of the Court was not along ideological lines. The majority opinion was authored by Chief Justice Roberts joined by justices Scalia, Ginsburg, Breyer and Kagan — an unlikely and unusual combination. According to the Chief Justice the failure of the state officials to appeal the trial court decision against them was the end of the matter. Writing for the minority, Justice Kennedy — joined by justices Alito, Thomas and Sotomayor — was concerned that merely by declining to contest the case, elected officials could bring about the nullification of laws sponsored by the voters. Kennedy wrote for the dissenting minority:

> What the Court fails to grasp is the basic premise of the initiative process. The essence of democracy is that the right to make law rests with the people and flows to the government, not the other way around. Freedom resides first in the people without need of a grant from government.

If California does become the thirteenth state to allow same-sex marriage, almost one-third of Americans will live in jurisdictions where it is legal. There has been a profound change in civil liberties for gay people in the last 2 years. As if to recognise this, in August 2013 Justice Ruth Bader Ginsburg became the first Supreme Court justice to officiate at a same-sex wedding.

Questions

1 What is an affirmative action programme?
2 How had the Supreme Court's membership changed since it last ruled on an affirmative action programme in 2003?
3 What was the Court's decision in *Fisher* v *University of Texas*?
4 Analyse the different reactions to this decision as presented in Box 3.1.
5 How did the supporters of affirmative action react to the decision?
6 Explain Sections 5 and 4(b) of the 1965 Voting Rights Act.
7 What did the Supreme Court say about these two sections of the Act in *Shelby County* v *Holder*?
8 Summarise the opinions of (a) Chief Justice Roberts and (b) Justice Ginsburg in this case.
9 Explain President Obama's reaction to this decision.
10 What effect did the Court's decision in *United States* v *Windsor* have on the Defense of Marriage Act?
11 What effect did the Court's decision in *Hollingsworth* v *Perry* have on California's ban on same-sex marriage?
12 How do these four decisions show the effect that the Supreme Court can have on rights and liberties in America?

US Government & Politics

Chapter 4

The Supreme Court: the 2012–13 term

What you need to know

- The Supreme Court is the highest federal court in the USA.
- The Court is made up of nine justices, appointed by the president, for life.
- Of the current nine justices, five were appointed by Republican presidents and four by Democrats.
- The Supreme Court has the power of judicial review. This is the power to declare acts of Congress or actions of the executive branch — or acts or actions of state governments — unconstitutional, and thereby null and void.
- By this power of judicial review, the Court acts as the umpire of the constitution and plays a leading role in safeguarding Americans' rights and liberties.

This chapter updates the material in the textbook (Anthony J. Bennett, *A2 US Government and Politics*, 4th edition, 2013) on the Supreme Court in Chapter 7.

The 78 opinions

In Chapter 3 we discussed and analysed the four landmark decisions handed down by the Supreme Court in its 2012–13 term. But these were only four of 78 opinions handed down by the Court during the term which ran from October 2012 to June 2013. That's pretty much par for the course in recent terms with the average number of opinions during the last 13 terms (since 2000) being 79. But as Figure 4.1 shows, this is significantly fewer than was the case during much of the mid- and late-twentieth century. Of these 78 cases, 66 (85%) came from the United States Courts of Appeals while the remaining 12 (15%) came from the state courts.

In discussing and analysing the most important and controversial cases we inevitably tend to concentrate mostly on close decisions — often those decided by 5 votes to 4. But most cases are not like that. In the 2012–13 term, 49% of cases were decided unanimously. This shows a significant and steady increase in the percentage of unanimous decisions over the past six terms as is shown in Table 4.1. A higher level of unanimity was a declared aim of Chief Justice Roberts when he took office in 2005. But as Table 4.1 also shows, the 5–4 decisions accounted for 29%, the highest figure for four terms. Indeed, the average over the last four terms has been just 22%. And, as we saw in Chapter 3, three of the four landmark decisions were decided on a 5–4 vote.

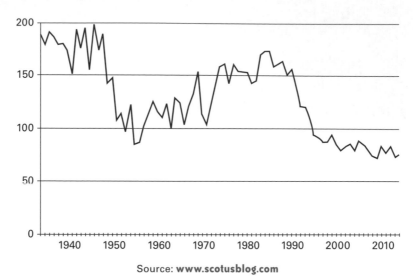

Source: www.scotusblog.com

Figure 4.1 Opinions handed down by Supreme Court, 1933–2013

Table 4.1 Unanimous and 5–4 decisions: 2007–13

Term	2007–08	2008–09	2009–10	2010–11	2011–12	2012–13
Number of decisions	67	74	86	80	75	78
% which were unanimous	30%	33%	46%	48%	44%	49%
% which were 5–4 decisions	17%	31%	19%	20%	20%	29%

Some decisions took longer to reach than others. The average length of time between oral argument and the announcement of the Court's opinion was 95 days. The shortest was 26 days — the 9–0 decision in *Metrish* v *Lancaster*. The longest was 257 days in the 7–1 decision in *Fisher* v *University of Texas*, the landmark decision about affirmative action where a complicated compromise had to be worked out between the justices. Furthermore, some justices work quicker than others. Justice Ruth Bader Ginsburg was the quickest worker this term, averaging just 60 days to write her opinions, while the slowest was Justice Anthony Kennedy who took almost twice as long — averaging 119 days. Not surprisingly, the 257-day wait for the decision in *Fisher* was a wait for a Kennedy-authored opinion.

Ruth agrees with Elena, but not with Sam

With the departure of David Souter in 2009 and of John Paul Stevens in 2010, the two new Obama appointees are now beginning to make their mark on the Court. The Souter and Stevens departures have probably left Clinton appointee Ruth Bader Ginsburg as the most reliably liberal voice on the Court and Obama's second appointee, Elena Kagan, seems to be allying herself closely to Ginsburg. The two were the justices most often in agreement with one another during the 2012–13 term, agreeing as they did in 96% of all decisions (see Table 4.2). At the other end of the scale, the two justices least often in agreement were Ginsburg and George W. Bush appointee Samuel Alito. They voted together on only 41% of cases and disagreed on all the 5–4 decisions issued during this term. Ginsburg and Alito were the two most frequently in disagreement in the 2010–11 term as well. For the past two terms, Ginsburg had been the justice most often in the minority, but she surrendered that position to Antonin Scalia in this term.

Table 4.2 Agreement and disagreement between justices: 2007–13

Term	2007–08	2008–09	2009–10	2010–11	2011–12	2012–13
Two justices most in agreement	Roberts Scalia	Roberts Alito	Ginsburg Sotomayor	Roberts Alito	Scalia Thomas	Ginsburg Kagan
Two justices most in disagreement	Thomas Stevens	Thomas Stevens	Thomas Stevens	Alito Ginsburg	Scalia Ginsburg	Alito Ginsburg

The Roberts Court or the Kennedy Court?

Tradition has it to name the Court after the incumbent chief justice. Thus we have had the Warren Court (Chief Justice Earl Warren, 1953–69), the Burger Court (Warren Burger, 1969–86) and the Rehnquist Court (William Rehnquist, 1986–2005). Therefore the period from 2005 to the present day is correctly referred to as that of the Roberts Court — John Roberts being the chief justice since his appointment to that position by President George W. Bush almost 9 years ago.

But there is another way of naming the Court — naming it after the most influential justice of the time who may or may not be the chief justice. Thus during much of the period officially known as that of the Rehnquist Court, the Supreme Court was referred to by some commentators as the O'Connor Court signifying that Justice Sandra Day O'Connor, rather than the chief justice, was the most influential member of the Court. In a court composed of four conservative justices and four liberals, O'Connor was a moderate conservative who could be persuaded to join with the liberal quartet on certain important cases such as affirmative action and abortion rights. This often made her the 'swing justice', swinging from the conservative to the liberal side in some — often landmark — decisions.

Since O'Connor's retirement in 2005 — the same year in which Chief Justice Rehnquist died — her role of swing justice has been taken up by Justice Anthony Kennedy. O'Connor's replacement was a truly conservative justice, Samuel Alito. There was no chance of him becoming the swing justice. So Anthony Kennedy, another moderate conservative, has during the past decade become the most influential justice on the Court.

How do we judge influence? Clearly one has influence on the Court if you are the justice who most frequently can persuade at least four of your colleagues to agree with your position. For once you have four plus yourself, you have a Supreme Court majority and your view on that particular case will be the one that will prevail. We can further refine this criterion by asking two additional questions: who is the justice most frequently in the majority in 5–4 decisions, and who is the justice most frequently in the majority in landmark decisions? Table 4.3 can help us answer these questions.

Table 4.3 Justice(s) most in the majority: 2007–13

Term	2007–08	2008–09	2009–10	2010–11	2011–12	2012–13
Justice(s) most in the majority	Roberts	Kennedy	Kennedy Roberts	Kennedy	Kennedy	Kennedy
Justice(s) most in majority in 5–4 decisions	Kennedy Thomas	Kennedy	Kennedy Thomas Scalia	Kennedy	Kennedy	Kennedy

First then, which justice has been most frequently in the majority during each of these six terms? As Table 4.3 shows, the answer is Anthony Kennedy — four times plus a fifth jointly with John Roberts. If one also includes the 2005–06 and 2006–07 terms, that statistic increases to six out of eight terms. In 2012–13, Kennedy was in the majority in 71 of the 78 decisions, which represents a 91% success rate. Indeed, this was the fifth consecutive term in which Kennedy was in the majority in over 90% of the decisions — quite a record.

Table 4.4 Justices in the majority in landmark decisions: 2006–13

Landmark decisions (year)	Court split	Justices in the majority
Hamdan v *Rumsfeld* (2006)	5–3	**Stevens,** Breyer Ginsburg, Souter, Kennedy
Gonzales v *Carhart* (2007)	5–4	**Kennedy,** Roberts, Alito, Thomas, Scalia
Parents Involved v *Seattle* (2007)	5–4	**Roberts,** Scalia, Thomas, Alito, Kennedy
District of Columbia v *Heller* (2008)	5–4	**Scalia,** Roberts, Thomas, Alito, Kennedy
Baze v *Rees* (2008)	7–2	**Roberts,** Breyer, Ginsburg, Stevens, Souter, Alito, Kennedy
Boumediene v *Bush* (2008)	5–4	**Kennedy,** Stevens, Souter, Ginsburg, Breyer

Landmark decisions (year)	Court split	Justices in the majority
Citizens United v *FEC* (2010)	5–4	**Roberts,** Scalia, Thomas, Alito, Kennedy
NFIB v *Sebelius* (2012)	5–4	**Roberts,** Ginsburg, Breyer, Sotomayor, Kagan
Arizona v *United States* (2012)	5–3	**Kennedy,** Roberts, Breyer, Ginsburg, Sotomayor
Fisher v *Texas* (2013)	7–1	**Kennedy,** Roberts, Alito, Thomas, Scalia, Sotomayor, Breyer

Bold = author of majority opinion

Second, which justice has been most frequently in the majority in 5–4 decisions during each of these six terms? The answer again is Anthony Kennedy. Table 4.3 shows that Kennedy has held this distinction in all six terms — four times on his own and twice jointly with Clarence Thomas and once also with Antonin Scalia. If one also includes again the 2005–06 and 2006–07 terms, that statistic increases to eight out of eight, again quite a record.

Third, which justice has been most frequently in the majority in landmark decisions during this period? We are here making a somewhat subjective decision on what constitutes a landmark ruling, but Table 4.4 shows what many neutral commentators would probably agree were the landmark decisions of the Court over the past eight terms.

Of the ten landmark decisions identified in Table 4.4, the justice most frequently in the majority was yet again Anthony Kennedy — in nine of them, all except the 2012 healthcare decision in which Kennedy authored the minority opinion. Not only was Justice Kennedy the most frequently in the majority, he also authored more landmark opinions — four of the ten — than any justice other than Roberts, who also authored four. Kennedy has therefore authored landmark decisions concerning abortion, executive power, immigration and affirmative action, and has also been in the majority in landmark decisions on gun control, capital punishment and campaign finance, again, quite a record. No wonder many prefer to call this the Kennedy Court.

Roberts: sports umpire or landscape gardener?

But there is another side to this question. Anthony Kennedy is an appointee of President Ronald Reagan. He joined the Court in 1988 and has just completed his 25th year in office. In 2 years' time he will be 80. By sharp contrast, John Roberts is an appointee of President George W. Bush. He joined the Court in 2005 and has just completed his 8th year in office. He's still in his 50s. During his confirmation hearings, Roberts famously likened American society to a sports field with himself and his fellow justices as the umpires.

Judges are like umpires. Umpires don't make the rules; they apply them. The role of an umpire and a judge is critical. They make sure everybody plays by the rules. But it is a limited role. Nobody ever went to a ball game to see the umpire.

It all sounded like the model of judicial modesty and restraint. But is that how things are turning out?

In his end of term commentary on the Court's 2012–13 term in the *New York Times*, Adam Liptak suggested a different metaphor for Chief Justice Roberts's role:

The more meaningful way to look at the court is as a movie, one starring Chief Justice John Roberts as a canny strategist with a tough side and his eyes on the horizon.

The court in 2013 may be the Kennedy Court, but Kennedy's days are numbered. He probably has only five or so more years to serve. His best days are behind him. Not so the chief. Roberts could well expect to still be chief justice at the beginning of the 2030s. He would still be younger than Kennedy is today. Roberts can afford to keep his eyes on the distant horizon. Or to change the metaphor yet again, Kennedy is the aged gardener planting annuals because he may not be around long enough to enjoy anything that takes longer to grow. Roberts is the landscape gardener, planting saplings today and who will still be around to see the trees in future decades. Roberts is playing the long game — prepared to make concessions, even accept defeats today, in order to lay the seeds for victories tomorrow. Here are three examples of Roberts as landscape gardener.

Back in 2009, Chief Justice Roberts wrote the majority opinion in *Northwest Austin Municipal Utility District No. 1* v *Holder*. This was an 8–1 decision in a case involving the constitutionality of the 1965 Voting Rights Act. The decision was one which was pleasing to those of a liberal political philosophy. But the price which Roberts exacted from the Court's liberal quartet in order to bring more conservative justices on board and thereby form a majority was precisely the language which Roberts used in 2013 to ensure the 5–4 decision in *Shelby County* v *Holder*. This was the decision we analysed in Chapter 3 which seems likely to ensure that the Act's centrepiece — Section 5 — will become a dead duck. An initial victory for the Court's liberals led to a later but much more significant victory for the Court's conservatives.

Then in 2012, Roberts sided with the Court's liberal quartet in the 'Obamacare' case of *National Federation of Independent Businesses* v *Sebelius*. The judgement was seen by most observers as a defeat for those of a conservative political philosophy. But in seeming to deliver a victory for liberals, Roberts had planted another seed — the part of the decision that restricted Congress's usage of the Constitution's commerce clause — which could yield a conservative harvest in years to come. As we commented in last year's update, this was 'mostly a liberal decision based on mostly conservative principles'. The decision applied only to Obamacare; the principles could be used for countless other judgements yet to come.

Finally, in 2013, in the *Fisher* v *University of Texas* decision (again, see Chapter 3 for the details), Chief Justice Roberts planted some more conservative seeds in a decision which was essentially a liberal–conservative compromise. By getting two liberal justices — Stephen Breyer and Sonia Sotomayor — to sign up to the 7–1 decision, Roberts got a result that could in future years restrict race-conscious admissions programmes at American universities. That would be a significant restricting of affirmative action and a victory for conservatives. As Adam Liptak concluded, Chief Justice Roberts is writing decisions which are like 'a conservative time bomb, but with a very long fuse'. But then like the landscape gardener the chief has time on his side.

What of the future?

Ruth Bader Ginsburg, appointed to the Court by President Clinton in 1993, is the oldest member of the Court. She will turn 81 early in 2014. Despite having suffered numerous health scares, she has talked frequently of her determination to remain on the Court for as long as she can. Oliver Wendell Holmes holds the record for the oldest serving justice. Appointed to the Court in 1902 aged 61 by President Theodore Roosevelt, he served 29 years before retiring in 1932 at the age of 90. In an interview with the *New York Times* in August 2013, Justice Ginsburg said that as long as her health and intellect remained strong she would want to remain fully engaged in the work of the Court, describing herself as the 'leader of the liberal opposition on one of the most activist courts in history'.

But the intriguing question is whether she will retire during the remaining years of Obama's second term or risk having her replacement named by a Republican president who might follow Obama at the White House. Given that Ginsburg is widely regarded as the most reliably liberal voice on the Court, were she to be replaced by a conservative justice, as would be likely if a Republican president were to name her successor, the ideological balance of the Court would be changed significantly. And what if that same Republican president serving in the years between 2017 and 2021 were also to name Anthony Kennedy's successor? One could then envisage a Supreme Court with six reliably conservative votes. Now there are a lot of 'ifs' in this paragraph, but it sets up some intriguing possibilities. My hunch is that Justice Ginsburg will retire within the next 2 years allowing Obama to name her successor. But the later she leaves it, the greater the likelihood that her successor may have to be confirmed by a Republican-controlled Senate.

Questions

1 What does Figure 4.1 show about the number of opinions handed down by the Supreme Court in the last 80 years?
2 Analyse the data presented in Table 4.1.
3 What do the data in Table 4.2 tell us about Justice Ruth Bader Ginsburg?
4 What evidence is presented for suggesting that the Supreme Court today is rightly referred to as 'the Kennedy Court'?
5 How influential has Justice Anthony Kennedy been in landmark decisions of the Court since 2006?
6 Explain Adam Liptak's comment on Chief Justice John Roberts that he is 'a canny strategist' who has 'his eyes on the horizon'.
7 Why is there particular interest in the retirement plans of Justice Ginsburg?
8 What could happen to the Court if a future *Republican* president were to name the replacements of both Justices Ginsburg and Kennedy?

Chapter 5

Just how partisan has Congress become, and why?

What you need to know

- Partisanship is a term used to denote a state of affairs in which members of one party regularly group together in opposition to the members of another party.

- Partisanship is therefore typified by high levels of party discipline, frequent occurrences of party-line voting, and little if any cooperation and compromise between politicians of different parties.

This chapter updates the material in the textbook (Anthony J. Bennett, *A2 US Government and Politics*, 4th edition, 2013) on political parties on pages 123–28 and on Congress on pages 216–19.

The way things were

Time was when American political parties were seemingly indistinguishable. Both parties seemed to encompass almost a complete cross-section of liberals and conservatives. There were liberal Democrats like Senator Edward Kennedy of Massachusetts and conservative Democrats like Lloyd Bentsen of Texas. There were conservative Republicans like Strom Thurmond of South Carolina — who used to be a Democrat — and liberal Republicans like Mark Hatfield of Oregon. This was the era in which the late Clinton Rossiter famously described America's two major parties as 'creatures of compromise, coalitions of interest, in which principle is muted and often silenced'. In Rossiter's view, the Democratic and Republican parties were like 'two vast, gaudy, friendly umbrellas, under which all Americans are invited to stand'. One can hardly imagine a description more unlike what we see today in American politics. 'Compromise', 'coalitions', 'principle muted and often silenced'? Today's Democrats and Republicans are more noted for their partisanship, confrontation, and ideological purity than for those characteristics of which Rossiter wrote some decades ago.

In the period between 1975 and 1993 — encompassing the presidencies of Gerald Ford, Jimmy Carter, Ronald Reagan and the first George Bush — Washington *was* a place of compromise. Legislation often passed through Congress with large bipartisan majorities. In teaching during this period, I would tell my students that a typical vote in Congress was 'a large group of Democrats and Republicans voting against a smaller group of Democrats and Republicans'. Members of Congress were noted for their 'working *across* the aisle' — a reference to the centre aisle which divides the Democrats from Republicans in both chambers of Congress. In other words, Democrats worked with Republicans, and vice versa.

And it was a similar picture when it came to voting at election time. Many voters would 'split their tickets' — voting, for example, for a Republican presidential candidate but a Democratic member of the House at the same election. The first House member I spent time with in Washington in the 1980s was Congressman Charles Bennett (no relative) — a Florida Democrat. But in both 1980 and 1984, the vast majority of Bennett's constituents in Florida's Third District not only re-elected him — a Democrat — to the House, but also voted for Republican Ronald Reagan in the presidential race. Bennett was an old style conservative Democrat. He had a lot in common with Ronald Reagan — certainly more than with liberal Walter Mondale who stood for the Democrats in the 1984 presidential election. But as we shall see, all this too has changed.

The Senate: 30 years of change

One of the simplest ways to understand what has happened to the Democrats and Republicans in Congress is to take a snapshot of the Senate in 1982 and again 30 years later in 2012 and see just how much things have changed. Back in 1982, one of the most liberal Senate Democrats was Edward Kennedy of Massachusetts. Meanwhile, the most conservative of the Senate Democrats was Ed Zorinsky of Nebraska. They rarely voted together, yet they belonged to the same party.

Among Senate Republicans in 1982, the most liberal was Lowell Weicker of Connecticut, but he was in the same party as the arch-conservative Strom Thurmond of South Carolina. Again, Weicker and Thurmond, although in the same party, had little in common and rarely voted the same way. Between Weicker (the most liberal Republican) and Zorinsky (the most conservative Democrat) were 35 Democrats and 23 Republicans. In other words, 35 Democrats were more conservative than Weicker, and 23 Republicans were more liberal than Zorinsky. Put yet another way, there was a group of Senate centrists made up of 58 senators — more than half the chamber. As Figure 5.1 shows, there was a huge ideological overlap between the two parties. The differences *within* the parties were far greater than the differences *between* them.

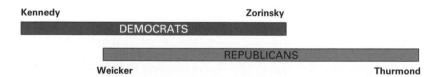

Figure 5.1 The parties in the Senate: 1982

Now let's jump forward 30 years to 2012 and take another snapshot of the Senate. In 2012, the most liberal Senate Democrat was Tom Udall of New Mexico. Meanwhile, the most conservative of the Senate Democrats was Joe Manchin of West Virginia. The most liberal Republican senator in 2012 was Scott Brown of Massachusetts, whilst the most conservative Republican in the Senate was Jim Risch of Idaho. But between Scott Brown (the most liberal Republican) and Joe

Manchin (the most conservative Democrat) there was not a single senator. In other words, all the Democrats were more liberal than Brown, and all the Republicans were more conservative than Manchin. The Senate centrists had gone. As Figure 5.2 shows, there was absolutely no ideological overlap at all between the two parties in the Senate in 2012. Now, the differences *between* the parties are greater than the differences *within*.

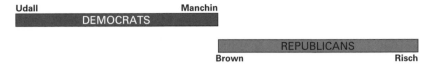

Figure 5.2 The parties in the Senate: 2012

The demise of the Senate centrists is a relatively recent phenomenon. As Table 5.1 shows, even as recently as 2003 and 2004, there were respectively 24 and 30 Senate centrists — Republicans who were more liberal than the most conservative Democrats, and Democrats who were more conservative than the most liberal Republican. The Senate took a sharp turn towards increased partisanship in 2005, during George W. Bush's second term, and now for the last 3 years — 2010, 2011 and 2012 — they have disappeared altogether.

Table 5.1 Number of centrist senators by party: 2003–12

Year	Number of Republicans more liberal than most conservative Democrat	Number of Democrats more conservative than most liberal Republican
2003	22	2
2004	28	2
2005	5	2
2006	8	2
2007	3	1
2008	2	3
2009	2	2
2010	0	0
2011	0	0
2012	0	0

The House: 20 years of change

Much the same change has occurred in the House of Representatives. Let's take two snapshots there — one in 1993, the first year of Bill Clinton's presidency, and another in 2012, the last year of George W. Bush's presidency. In 1993, the most liberal House Democrat was Ronald Dellums of California, while the most conservative House Democrat was Ralph Hall of Texas. Among House

Republicans the most liberal was Jim Leach of Iowa, while the most conservative was Tom DeLay of Texas. But between Leach (the most liberal Republican) and Hall (the most conservative Democrat) were 51 Democrats and 26 Republicans. Put another way, there was a group of House centrists made up of 79 members — almost one-fifth of the chamber.

There were some obvious geographic trends in these House centrists. Of the 52 most conservative House Democrats in 1993, 34 (65%) were from the South. Add in a further five from the border states of Oklahoma and Kentucky, and you reach 75%. Similarly, of the 28 most liberal House Republicans in 1993, 18 (64%) were from the Northeast and Mid-Atlantic states.

So what did the House look like by 2012? In that year, the most liberal House Republican was Chris Gibson of New York, while the most conservative House Democrat was Dan Boren of Oklahoma. But between Gibson and Boren there were just nine Democrats and four Republicans. In other words, the House centrists now numbered just 13 members — only 3% of the chamber.

Centrists replaced by ideologues

If one looks closely at recent congressional elections, one can see another significant trend, namely that a number of centrists have been replaced by ideologues. Moderate Democrats have been replaced by conservative Republicans, and moderate Republicans have been replaced by liberal Democrats.

Let's start in the Senate. In 2006, moderate Republican Lincoln Chafee lost to Democrat Sheldon Whitehouse. Senator Whitehouse was ranked the 19th most liberal senator in 2011. In the same year, moderate Republican Mike DeWine of Ohio lost to Democrat Sharrod Brown. Senator Brown was ranked the 5th most liberal senator in 2012. Then in 2008, another moderate Republican Gordon Smith of Oregon lost to Democrat Jeff Merkley who in 2011 was rated the most liberal member of the Senate. Also in 2008, another moderate Republican Norm Coleman of Minnesota lost to Democrat Al Franken who in 2012 was ranked the third most liberal member of the Senate. The same thing has happened with regard to moderate Democrats. In 2010, Senator Evan Bayh of Indiana retired and was replaced by a conservative Republican, Dan Coats. In 2012, Senator Ben Nelson of Nebraska retired and was replaced by a staunch conservative Republican Deb Fischer. No wonder the Senate has become more partisan.

The same pattern is seen in the House. Among the most conservative House Democrats back in 1993 were Mike Parker of Mississippi, Billy Tauzin of Louisiana and Charles Stenholm of Texas. Parker and Tauzin switched to become Republicans later that decade, but the House seats of all three are now occupied by staunchly conservative Republicans — respectively Steve Palazzo, Charles Boustany and Bill Flores. All those three House Republicans were ranked among the 40 most conservative House members in 2012.

Split districts (and states) on the decline

Split-ticket voting

The practice of voting for candidates of two or more parties for different offices at the same election. The opposite — voting for candidates of the same party for different offices at the same election — is called straight-ticket voting.

Another factor which used to promote bipartisanship was split-ticket voting. We've already come across Charles Bennett, a Democrat who represented Florida's Third Congressional District in the 1980s, whose constituents nonetheless voted overwhelmingly for Republican presidential candidate Ronald Reagan — twice. The effect of having people in the House and the Senate — Democrats whose constituents had voted Republican in the recent presidential election, or Republicans whose constituents had voted Democrat for president — was that such members of Congress were likely to be open to working and voting across the aisle. Bennett, for example, was among a large number of Democrats who voted for Reagan's tax cuts. Split-ticket voting encouraged bipartisanship.

Split district

A split district is a district — a geographic part of a state which elects a member of the House — which at the same election votes for a Republican for the House but Democrat in the presidential race, or vice versa. A split state is a state which at the same election votes for a Democrat for the Senate but Republican in the presidential race, or vice versa.

The opposite is also true. Straight-ticket voting encourages partisanship. And during the last two decades, the number of split districts — or if we're looking at the Senate, split states — has declined quite significantly. Let's start with the Senate by going back to 1976 — the year which saw the election of Democrat president Jimmy Carter when he defeated the incumbent, Republican Gerald Ford. There were Senate elections in 33 states that year — 22 contests were won by Democrats and 11 by Republicans. Table 5.2 shows, however, that in only 19 of these 33 contests did the state vote either Democrat or Republican in both the presidential and Senate elections. The other 14 were split states — ten which voted for Republican Gerald Ford for president but elected a Democrat to the Senate, and four which voted for Democrat Jimmy Carter for president but elected a Republican to the Senate. Thus 42% of these states ended up as split states.

Table 5.2 Presidential and senatorial elections, 1976: by party

Democrat president Democrat senator	Republican president Republican senator	Democrat president Republican senator	Republican president Democrat senator
Florida	California	Delaware	Arizona
Hawaii	Connecticut	Missouri	Maine
Maryland	Indiana	Pennsylvania	Michigan
Massachusetts	New Mexico	Rhode Island	Montana
Minnesota	Utah		Nebraska
Mississippi	Vermont		Nevada
New York	Wyoming		New Jersey
Ohio			North Dakota
Tennessee			Virginia
Texas			Washington
West Virginia			
Wisconsin			
12	7	4	10
19		14	

Now let's compare the elections of 1976 with those in 2012. That year there were Senate elections in the same 33 states — 21 contests were won by Democrats and 12 by Republicans. And with a Democrat winning the presidential race — as in 1976 — we can see that in these regards 1976 and 2012 are comparable. But Table 5.3 shows that in terms of split-ticket voting and the subsequent numbers of split states, 2012 was very different from 1976. What Table 5.3 shows is that in 27 of these 33 contests, the same party won both the presidential and senatorial elections. In only six states did different parties win these two elections. In other words, by 2012 the percentage of split states had fallen from 42% in 1976 to just 18%.

It is also worth noting that two of the states in column 4 — Indiana and Missouri — would almost certainly have been in column 2 had not the state Republican parties fielded somewhat loopy candidates. Furthermore, the Senate races in Nevada Montana and North Dakota were decided by less than two percentage points. So the number of split states could easily have been reduced to just one — West Virginia. Now here was an old-style split state. In the presidential race Romney beat Obama by 26 percentage points, while in the Senate race Democrat Joe Manchin beat his Republican opponent by 24 points. That's how things used to be. And remember who Joe Manchin was — the most conservative of the Senate Democrats in 2012.

Now if we widen this out to the whole Senate, let's compare 1977 and 2013 in answering this question: how many of the 100 senators in those years represented states that had voted for the other party in the preceding year's presidential election? In 1977, there were 41 — 28 Democrats from states that had voted for Republican Gerald Ford in 1976, and 13 Republicans from states that had voted for Democrat Jimmy Carter. By 2013, there were just 21 — 12 Democrats from states that had voted for Mitt Romney and nine Republicans from states that had voted for Barack Obama. Box 5.1 shows that seven of those 12 'Romney Democrats' are up for re-election in 2014, as is one of the nine 'Obama Republicans'. So this list might be even smaller by January 2015. But be that as it may, here is yet another factor which contributes to higher levels of partisanship in Congress.

Table 5.3 Presidential and senatorial elections, 2012: by party

Democrat president Democrat senator	Republican president Republican senator	Democrat president Republican senator	Republican president Democrat senator
California	Arizona	Nevada	Indiana
Connecticut	Mississippi		Missouri
Delaware	Nebraska		Montana
Florida	Tennessee		North Dakota
Hawaii	Texas		West Virginia
Maine	Utah		
Maryland	Wyoming		
Massachusetts			
Michigan			
Minnesota			
New Jersey			
New Mexico			
New York			
Ohio			
Pennsylvania			
Rhode Island			
Vermont			
Virginia			
Washington			
Wisconsin			
20	7	1	5
27		**6**	

Much the same pattern can be seen in the House of Representatives where split districts have declined dramatically over the past three decades. As Table 5.4 shows, 30 years ago, almost half of the members of the House came from split districts. They were either Republicans whose district had voted for Democrat Walter Mondale in 1984 or they were Democrats whose district had voted for President Reagan. After the 1984 election, just over 45% of House members fell into these two categories. But in 1988, the proportion fell to one-third and to less than a quarter in 1992. By 2000, it was down to a fifth. Thus when George W. Bush arrived in the White House there were only 86 House members from split districts.

Box 5.1 'Romney Democrats' and 'Obama Republicans' in the Senate, 2013–14

Democrat senators from Romney states	Republican senators from Obama states
†Mark Begich (Alaska)	Marco Rubio (Florida)
†Mark Pryor (Arkansas)	Mark Kirk (Illinois)
Joe Donnelly (Indiana)	Chuck Grassley (Iowa)
†Mary Landrieu (Louisiana)	†Susan Collins (Maine)
Claire McCaskill (Missouri)	Dean Heller (Nevada)
*†Max Baucus (Montana)	Kelly Ayotte (New Hampshire)
Jon Tester (Montana)	Rob Portman (Ohio)
†Kay Hagan (North Carolina)	Pat Toomey (Pennsylvania)
Heidi Heitkamp (North Dakota)	Ron Johnson (Wisconsin)
*†Tim Johnson (South Dakota)	(9)
†Jay Rockefeller (West Virginia)	
Joe Manchin (West Virginia)	
(12)	

† seat up for election in 2014
* not seeking re-election in 2014

Table 5.4 Split districts: 1980–2012

Year	Number of split districts	Percentage
1980	143	32.8
1984	196	45.1
1988	148	34.0
1992	100	23.0
1996	110	25.3
2000	86	19.8
2004	59	13.6
2008	83	19.1
2012	26	5.9

After the 2012 election, the figures had fallen again. During the 113th Congress (2013–14) when President Obama began his second term, there were just 26 House members — representing less than 6% of the total — who were from split districts. And as Box 5.2 shows, there were just 17 Republicans who came from districts who had voted for Obama in 2012.

But when we look more closely at these 17 Obama Republicans in the House, there's even more bad news for the President. In only one of these 17 districts — California 31 — did Obama get more than 55% of the vote. Furthermore, in 11 of them, he won less than 52% of the vote, indicating that his support in the district

Box 5.2	'Romney Democrats' and 'Obama Republicans' in the House, 2013–14	

Democrat House members from Romney districts	Republican House members from Obama districts
Ann Kirkpatrick (Arizona 1)	Jeff Denham (California 10)
Ron Barber (Arizona 2)	David Valadao (California 21)
Patrick Murphy (Florida 18)	Gary Miller (California 31)
John Barrow (Georgia 12)	Mike Coffman (Colorado 6)
Collin Peterson (Minnesota 7)	Bill Young (Florida 13)
Mike McIntyre (North Carolina 7)	Ileana Ros-Lehtinen (Florida 27)
Pete Gallego (Texas 23)	Tom Latham (Iowa 3)
Jim Matheson (Utah 4)	John Kline (Minnesota 2)
Nick Rahall (West Virginia 3)	Erik Paulsen (Minnesota 3)
(9)	Joe Heck (Nevada 3)
	Frank LoBiondo (New Jersey 2)
	Jon Runyan (New Jersey 3)
	Peter King (New York 2)
	Michael Grimm (New York 11)
	Chris Gibson (New York 19)
	Scott Rigell (Virginia 2)
	David Reichert (Washington 8)
	(17)

was somewhat underwhelming, hardly enough to convince a Republican to stick his neck out for the President in a tough vote on the floor of the House. And in only two districts — California 31 and Colorado 6 — did the President outpoll the Republican congressman. And in both districts, Obama outpolled the Republican congressman by just 2 percentage points.

What does it all mean?

At the start of this chapter we asked two interconnected questions: how partisan has Congress become, and why? We are now in a position to draw together answers to both of them. Figures 5.1 and 5.2 show how very partisan the Senate has become and Table 5.1 shows how very partisan the House has become. There are no longer any true 'centrists' left in either chamber. In the Senate there are no Republicans more liberal than a Democrat, and no Democrats more conservative than a Republican. The Democrats and Republicans in Congress now seem to line up just like the Conservative and Labour Party MPs used to line up in the UK House of Commons — with Prussian discipline. This makes life very difficult for a president who does not have his own party in the majority in both houses of Congress. In the 34 years between 1981 and 2014, a president has had his own party in control of both houses of Congress for only 8½ of those years — less than a quarter of the time: Bill Clinton for 2 years (1993–94); George W. Bush for 4½ years (part of 2001, and 2003–06); and Barack Obama for 2 years (2009–10).

For the remaining 25½ years presidents have either controlled only one chamber (11½ years) or neither (14 years). It is quite possible that the years 2015–16 will add a further 2 years to the latter category should the Republicans hold the House (very likely) and win the Senate (quite possible) in the 2014 mid-term elections.

Why has Congress become so partisan? There are actually many reasons — too many to be covered in one chapter here. But we have seen that a major factor is what Bill Bishop has called 'the big sort' (Bill Bishop, *The Big Sort: Why the Clustering of Like-Minded America is Tearing Us Apart*, Houghton Mifflin Company, 2008). States, and even congressional districts, are becoming ever 'redder' or 'bluer' — more staunchly Republican or Democrat. This has resulted, as we have seen, in the sharp decline of the split state and the split district. This leads to it being much more difficult for presidents to persuade members of Congress to vote across party lines. The results are increased partisanship in Congress, and greatly enfeebled presidents. We always used to say that 'the president's power is the power to persuade', but if there are so few who are persuadable, is this either relevant or true anymore?

Questions

1 Explain what has happened to the parties in the Senate in the last 30 years using Figures 5.1 and 5.2.
2 To what extent has the House of Representatives changed in terms of partisanship between 1993 and 2012?
3 Explain, with examples, what it means to say that in Congress 'centrists have been replaced by ideologues'.
4 What is (a) a split district and (b) a split state?
5 What do the data in Tables 5.2 and 5.3 tell us about the change in split states between 1976 and 2012?
6 Analyse the data presented in Table 5.4.
7 What is meant by (a) a Romney Democrat, and (b) an Obama Republican?
8 Why do the data presented in the right-hand column of Box 5.2 make life difficult for President Obama?
9 Why might it be outdated to still claim that 'the president's power is the power to persuade'?

Chapter 6

New media vs old media: which is now more influential?

What you need to know

- The term 'old media' generally refers to television, radio news, printed newspapers and magazines.
- The term 'new media' generally refers to electronic media and includes the internet, social networking sites such as Twitter and Facebook, as well as talk radio.

The way things were

In Chapter 5 we saw what a dramatic change has taken place both in the two major parties, and as a result in Congress, over the past three decades or so. In turning to look at the news and information media in America, we are playing the same tune — change — but just putting different words to it.

When I began visiting Washington DC about 35 years ago, the term 'the media' was limited in scope. In terms of television, one basically had a choice between the three terrestrial channels — ABC, CBS and NBC. Television news was dominated by the big beasts like Peter Jennings on ABC, Walter Cronkite and Dan Rather on CBS and John Chancellor on NBC. Then there were newspapers. In Washington almost everyone I knew seemed to read the *Washington Post*, almost iconic in the post-Watergate era. But there was the *Washington Times* for those who liked their news to come with a rather more conservative slant. The only other news sources available were the weeklies — most notably *Time* and *Newsweek*, but also *US News and World Report* for those who liked their politics a bit more in-depth. Quintessentially, this was the old media. It had existed for decades, and we had no idea that things were about to change quite so dramatically.

Change has come

The first changes came with the advent of cable television — a novelty to me during my first visits across the Atlantic. Whereas at that time in England I could receive only three television stations — BBC1, BBC2 and ITV — in America I could watch dozens. And cable television, having originally concentrated on sports and entertainment, eventually branched out into covering politics. C-SPAN — with its live, gavel to gavel, coverage of Congress — was launched in 1979 with coverage of the House of Representatives. They added C-SPAN2 in 1986 when the Senate

agreed to permit television cameras. Between those two launches, Cable News Network (CNN) arrived on American television screens in 1980.

But as Table 6.1 shows it was the 15 years from 1991 to 2006 that saw the biggest revolution in the way Americans — and people in all modern industrialised countries — garnered political information, and shared it with each other. It is extraordinary to think that in the election of 1992 which brought Bill Clinton to the White House — hardly ancient history — there was no e-mail, no Google, no blogging, no Facebook, no YouTube and no Twitter. Even the internet with its strange vocabulary of 'www dot', its 'coms' and 'orgs' was in its infancy.

Table 6.1 The arrival of 'new media'

1979	C-SPAN (House of Representatives)
1980	CNN
1986	C-SPAN2 (Senate)
1991	Internet: World Wide Web
1993	E-mail
1996	MSNBC, Fox News
1998	Google search engine
1999	Blogging
2001	C-SPAN3
2003	Skype
2004	Facebook; Podcasts
2005	YouTube
2006	Twitter

I still remember walking from my apartment on Q Street in Washington DC one day in 1994 and seeing a strange advertisement on the side of a local bus, inviting me to 'log on to www.washingtonpost.com' rather than buy my printed newspaper for 25 cents at the corner store. I had no idea what it meant. All these developments have occurred within the lifetime of all my student readers this year, born as you were in the mid-1990s. It is only the two Obama elections — 2008 and 2012 — which have featured YouTube and Twitter, and for which Facebook has been commonly available throughout.

Such stunning changes in the way people receive and communicate news — especially their political news and views — have had a profound effect on American politics. In this chapter, we take a look at what these changes are and what effect they have had on American politics in general and on presidential elections in particular. The organisation which researches this is the Pew Research Center. You can see its data at **www.people-press.org** and the rest of this chapter is based on some of its recently published research.

Watching, reading and listening to news

Table 6.2 shows that television and radio news as well as newspapers have all suffered a sharp decline in the past two decades. The sharpest decline has been in newspaper readership, down from 56% in 1992 to just 29% in 2012. The increases have come from new media that were not even in existence two decades ago. By 2012, nearly four in ten Americans got their news online or on a mobile device such as a phone or tablet. When other online digital news sources are added in — seeing news on social networking sites, Twitter, getting news by e-mail or listening to a podcast — the percentage goes up to 50%, almost the same as those who get their news from television. One could imagine that by the next presidential election in 2016, digital news will have replaced television news as the most popular medium.

But when we look at these figures by age group, we see how inevitable the change from 'old media' to 'new media' is becoming. Let's take that 55% from 2012 who told researchers that they watched news on television the previous day. Table 6.3 breaks this group down by age group. What we see is that whereas nearly three-quarters of seniors watched television news the previous day, only one-third of 18–29 year olds did so — a huge disparity. Table 6.3 also shows a significant drop off in the 18–29-year-old group's television news watching in the period between 2006 and 2012. Whereas in 2006, 49% of this age group said they watched television news, this had fallen by 15 percentage points by 2012.

Table 6.2 Where people got news yesterday: 1992 and 2012 compared

Where did you get news from yesterday?	1992	2012
Watched news on television	68%	55%
Read a newspaper	56%	29%
Listened to radio news	54%	33%
Online/mobile news	0%	39%
Any digital news	0%	50%

Table 6.3 Television news watching by age: 2006 and 2012 compared

Age group	2006 %	2012 %	Change
18–29	49	34	–15
30–49	53	52	–1
50–64	63	65	+2
65+	69	73	+4

Not only did newspaper readership fall, but so did magazine readership. As recently as 2008, there were still three weekly news magazines covering

American politics — *Time, Newsweek* and *US News and World Report.* In June 2008, *US News and World Report,* after 75 years as a weekly magazine, switched to biweekly publication, and then in November of the same year became a monthly. Two years later, it announced it was dropping its print version and continuing only as an online publication. *Newsweek* managed to keep going as a weekly magazine for 79 years, but finally — from January 2013 — succumbed to market forces and now appears only online. Well over half of the subscribers to the *New York Times* now subscribe to the online rather than the print version of the newspaper, myself included. *USA Today* and the *Wall Street Journal* are both heading the same way.

New media feels change too

While the old media has lost out and has tried to adapt to its falling market share, there have been changes too in the new media. Nearly one in five Americans now get their news on a mobile device, mostly on what Americans call their 'cell phone' — that's a 'mobile' in British English. Among smart phone owners, that figure rises to almost a third. But one in five Americans now get their news via social networking sites, up from one in ten just 3 years ago. Over half of Americans now access the internet via a mobile device — cell phone, tablet or the like. Among this group, 30% say they saw news on social networking sites in the last 24 hours.

While news gathering is very common among Twitter users, the overall reach is more limited than for cell phones or tablets because the audience remains significantly smaller. By 2012, only around 13% of Americans were Twitter users. By comparison, over half (54%) were using other social networking sites such as Facebook, Google Plus or LinkedIn.

Trends in the 2012 campaign

At the very start of the 2012 presidential campaign, the Pew Research Center conducted a survey to find out how different age groups were finding out about the campaign — both that for the President's re-nomination as well as for the Republican race. People were offered a number of different sources — both old media and new — from which they might regularly learn something about the campaigns. Table 6.4 shows the survey's findings.

The first thing to observe from this table is how few under 30s were regularly learning about the campaign from any source. Even the internet attracted less than one-third of this age group on a regular basis, though it was their most popular source of regular information. The only old media more popular with the under 30s than the over 65s was late night comedy shows — the under 30s fourth most popular source of regular campaign information.

In terms of the really old media — local and national television news and local newspapers — there was a huge difference between young people and seniors, with local television news being three times more popular with seniors as a source of regular campaign information as compared with under 30s. Likewise, the internet was almost three times more popular with under 30s than with seniors. This shows clearly the age-based old–new media divide.

Table 6.4 Regular source of campaign information (2012): by age group

Regularly learn something about campaign from...	18–29 years %	30–49 years %	50–64 years %	65+ years %	Old–young difference
Old media					
Local television news	15	33	37	45	+30
National nightly network news	12	21	37	36	+24
Local daily newspaper	11	18	24	31	+20
Cable news networks	28	32	39	47	+19
Cable news talk shows	11	7	19	28	+17
Morning television news shows	9	12	21	23	+14
Sunday morning talk shows	4	10	19	15	+11
Late night comedy shows	15	7	9	6	−9
New media					
Websites/apps of news organisations	17	23	22	14	−3
YouTube videos	5	3	2	1	−4
Twitter	4	2	1	0	−4
Online websites/apps	13	14	12	5	−8
Facebook	11	8	4	1	−10
The internet	29	33	21	11	−18

Conclusions

We often focus on *political* divides when we talk about the media — Republicans watching Fox and Democrats watching MSNBC; Republicans reading the *Wall Street Journal* and Democrats reading the *New York Times*. The trouble is these are only caricatures and they are based only on old media habits. What we have seen from this chapter is that the *age* divide is more significant than the political divide. And the age divide shows a clear tendency towards old media in the older age groups and towards new media in the younger.

When we see partisan and philosophical differences between the age groups, we often have to keep in mind that people may change their partisan or philosophical preferences as they get older. But with regard to the media, it seems a pretty sure thing that today's under 30s will not suddenly start watching the nightly network news in large numbers as they get older. Neither will they stop using the internet

or downloading news apps, and swap e-mails and Facebook for more traditional means of communication. Given the changes in the new media over the past 15 years, it is impossible to say how Americans will be getting their political and campaign news in another 15 years. What, after all, will the media look like in 2030? But one thing seems certain, the old media will continue to decline.

Questions

1 To what does the term 'old media' refer? Give some examples.
2 What does Table 6.1 tell us about the way media have changed over the past 35 years?
3 What does Table 6.2 tell us about the changes in the way Americans get their news between 1992 and 2012?
4 What does Table 6.3 tell us about the relationship between age and watching television news?
5 What evidence does the chapter give of the decline of print journalism?
6 What changes have occurred in the 'new media'?
7 Analyse the data in Table 6.4.
8 What does the chapter conclude about the possible fate of old media?

Chapter 7

What makes President Obama's job so difficult?

What the Founding Fathers wanted

For anyone who thinks that the president is 'the most powerful man in the world', the question that forms the title to this chapter will seem more than a little strange. How can one have the words 'president', 'job' and 'difficult' in the same sentence, and for it still to make sense? But even as far back as the 1960s, President Lyndon Johnson was heard to bewail 'The only power I've got is nuclear, and I'm not allowed to use that!' It's probably true to say that except in those very rare moments of world crisis — Truman's authorisation of the atomic bomb attacks on Japan in 1945, Kennedy's eyeball-to-eyeball encounter with Soviet president Khrushchev in 1962 — the American presidency has never been particularly powerful, and the president has never been the 'most powerful man in the world' — possibly not even in America. And this was not because of any deficiency on behalf of the 43 men who have thus far held the office, but because the Founding Fathers back in the eighteenth century designed it that way. They deliberately created a presidency that was limited, that was hedged about with all kinds of checks and balances. One could almost say that they designed the presidency in such a way that it wouldn't work — and they were mightily successful.

All that said, recent-day presidents, especially the last three holders of the office — Bill Clinton, George W. Bush and Barack Obama — have had a more difficult time than many of their predecessors. The reason for this is because the political environment in which they have had to operate is less conducive to presidential success than it was for say Franklin Roosevelt or Harry Truman back in the middle of the last century.

One more thing before we proceed with the answer. Is the question accurate in its assumption? Has Barack Obama had a difficult time as president? Now of course, we're not suggesting he's not had his successes. He has managed to get some impressive pieces of legislation passed through Congress. He has received Senate approval to make significant appointments to both the executive and judicial branches of the federal government. He did win re-election in 2012. But it is beyond question that whatever victories Obama has achieved have come at a price — of much time, effort and persuasion. And there are a number of things he would have wanted to achieve — gun control legislation, immigration reform, and the closure of the detention camp at Guantanamo Bay to mention but three — where he has signally failed to get his way with Congress. So what makes his job so difficult? Let's consider five factors.

His less than overwhelming mandate at the last election

True, Barack Obama achieved what Gerald Ford in 1976, Jimmy Carter in 1980 and the first George Bush in 1992 failed to achieve — he *was* re-elected to a second term. But then of the 31 presidents who have run for re-election, only nine have lost. So getting re-elected was not all that surprising. In itself it brings little political clout.

But there were clear weaknesses in Obama's re-election. He became the first president since Woodrow Wilson in 1916 to be re-elected with a smaller number of Electoral College votes than in his first election. Table 7.1 shows that since Wilson's re-election in 1916, seven presidents have been re-elected to a second term, all, with the exception of Obama, with a higher electoral vote the second time around.

Table 7.1 Electoral College votes: difference between first and second elections, 1932–2012

President	First election	Second election	Difference
Franklin Roosevelt	472	523	+51
Dwight Eisenhower	442	457	+15
Richard Nixon	301	520	+219
Ronald Reagan	489	525	+36
Bill Clinton	370	379	+9
George W. Bush	271	286	+15
Barack Obama	365	332	−33

Obama's 2012 re-election also marked another undistinguished 'first'. He became the first president since Ulysses Grant in 1872 to be re-elected to a second consecutive term with a smaller share of the popular vote than in his first election. Table 7.2 shows that of the nine presidents re-elected to a consecutive second term since 1872, Obama was the only one to fail to increase his share of the popular vote, seeing it fall by just under 2 percentage points. This compared with an average popular vote increase of just over 6 percentage points for his eight re-elected predecessors.

Table 7.2 Popular vote (%): difference between first and second elections, 1896–2012

President	First election	Second election	Difference
William McKinley	51.0	51.6	+0.6
Woodrow Wilson	41.9	49.3	+7.4
Franklin Roosevelt	57.4	60.8	+3.4
Dwight Eisenhower	55.1	57.4	+2.3
Richard Nixon	43.4	60.7	+17.3
Ronald Reagan	50.7	58.8	+8.1
Bill Clinton	42.3	49.2	+6.9
George W. Bush	47.9	50.7	+2.8
Barack Obama	52.9	51.1	−1.8

This may all sound a bit like geeky statistics for the American politics 'anorak'. But they're far more than that. Consider President Reagan's position in his second term in the 1980s. He had been re-elected with almost 59% of the popular vote. He had won 49 of the 50 states and 525 of the 538 electoral votes. His 59% of the popular vote was higher than a good many members of Congress had received in their states or districts. He could claim a mandate. In comparison, Obama won only 26 states and just 332 electoral votes. His share of the vote at 51% was lower than most members of Congress had received in their states or districts. As a result, Obama can claim very little in the way of a mandate during his second term. And that leads us to a second factor.

It's his second — and last — term

Second terms are rarely political success stories. Think Richard Nixon and Watergate; think Bill Clinton and impeachment; think George W. Bush and Iraq, along with economic collapse. Indeed, second terms are often so calamitous, one wonders why any president bothers to seek one.

> ### Presidential support score
>
> An annual statistic measuring how often the president won in recorded votes in the House and the Senate on which he took a clear position, expressed as a percentage of the whole.

Take two measures — one of success, the other of popularity. Take the four presidents who have completed two full terms since the Second World War — Dwight Eisenhower (1953–61), Ronald Reagan (1981–89), Bill Clinton (1993–2001) and George W. Bush (2001–09). Over the 32 years of those four presidencies, their average support score in Congress was 65.6%. But in Table 7.3 we separate first terms and second terms. Including Obama's scores, we see that the average presidential support score for these five presidents in their first terms was 74.2% and all five scored above the overall average of 65.6%. But in the second terms, all four presidents registered a significantly lower average — Reagan and Bush by over 20 percentage points. Furthermore, the second term average was over 17 percentage points lower than the first term average. No president reached the 65.6% overall average score in his second term. One would therefore expect Obama's second term support score to come in somewhere around 56%, lower than both Eisenhower and Bush.

Table 7.3 Presidential support score averages: first and second terms compared

President	First term average (%)	Second term average (%)	Difference
Dwight Eisenhower	78.1	65.3	−12.8
Ronald Reagan	71.9	51.7	−20.2
Bill Clinton	66.1	49.3	−16.8
George W. Bush	81.5	61.3	−20.2
Barack Obama	73.4	–	–
Average	**74.2**	**56.9**	**−17.3**

Not only does a president's success rate in Congress usually decline in his second term, so does his approval rating with the public at large. Table 7.4 shows that the average first term approval rating for the eight presidents since 1945 who have gone on to a second term — this table includes Truman, Johnson and Nixon, who each served incomplete terms — was 58.3%. But in their second terms this dipped by over 10 percentage points to just 47.7%, with only Reagan and Clinton bucking the trend. By the autumn of 2013, Gallup was even reporting a significant decline in Obama's approval rating among Democrats — down from 91% in December 2012 to just 78% 10 months later.

Table 7.4 Presidential approval rating averages: first and second terms compared

President	First term average (%)	Second term average (%)	Difference
Harry Truman	55.6†	36.5	−19.1
Dwight Eisenhower	69.6	60.5	−9.1
Lyndon Johnson	74.2†	50.3	−23.9
Richard Nixon	55.8	34.4†	−21.4
Ronald Reagan	50.3	55.3	+5.0
Bill Clinton	49.6	60.6	+11.0
George W. Bush	62.2	36.5	−25.7
Barack Obama	49.0	–	–
Average	**58.3**	**47.7**	**−10.6**

† incomplete terms

Part of the problem here is the second term malaise resulting from the Twenty-Second Amendment, passed in 1951, limiting presidents to two terms. Second term presidents quickly become lame ducks as the focus of Washington politics becomes more to do with their likely successor. They soon become 'yesterday's men'. Second term presidents find it increasingly difficult to attract men and women of talent to serve in their administrations, either in the White House or in the cabinet. Folk who have already served four or more years often run out of steam — and ideas. The term 'exhausted volcanoes' comes to mind — a term first used in 1874 by British politician Benjamin Disraeli in reference to William Gladstone's administration which by then had been in office for 6 years.

Something else which often becomes more noticeable during second terms is dysfunction between the White House and the cabinet departments and agencies. Here's how one commentator summed up things as Obama began his second term:

> In some areas the White House had become almost dysfunctional. Relations with Cabinet-level departments were so tangled that it was often hard to get decisions made. The White House staff had become so big and arrogant that it was tripping over itself and driving the agencies crazy.

Examples were many. The department of transportation, for example, was never asked if the $48 billion which was included in the economic stimulus legislation was really enough for infrastructure projects. They needed three times the amount. And the housing and urban development secretary Shaun Donovan was heard to remark that on big housing decisions, his department was 'sat at the children's table'.

Second terms also seem to be more prone to scandals than first terms — Nixon and Watergate, Reagan and Iran–Contra, Clinton and Lewinsky, the second Bush and Iraq. The reason here is probably best thought of in terms of chickens coming home to roost. The second term scandals are often the result of weaknesses and behaviour which was evident in the first term but which, shall we say, matures in the second term: Nixon's secrecy and paranoia, Reagan's hands-off approach to policy-making, Clinton's sexual peccadilloes, and Bush's lack of curiosity. Had they served only one term, the results of these weaknesses would not have had time to show themselves so obviously. Which leads us to ask the question: what are Obama's behavioural weaknesses that might lead to second term problems?

Personal weaknesses

Like any fallible human being — which I think includes everyone — Barack Obama has his weaknesses. As Jonathan Alter has noted, 'he doesn't much like the public parts of the presidency' (*The Center Holds: Obama and His Enemies*, Simon & Schuster, 2013). This shows itself in two ways. First, when in Washington, Obama dislikes rubbing shoulders with 'hordes' of members of Congress at White House 'functions'. He is happy to do one-on-ones, but rather in the mould of Jimmy Carter, somewhat resents having to do congressional bun fights just to bolster congressional egos. Second, when away from the White House, Obama dislikes working rope lines of admirers or supporters. He will turn up at a function and give the speech — usually rather well — but, unlike Bill Clinton, he is not one to hang around afterwards and press the flesh, sign autographs and pose for pictures. As Alter commented, 'Obama didn't do himself any favours by undervaluing the importance of personal relationships in getting things done in Washington.'

This almost Nixonesque love of personal privacy also comes across in another way which hinders him politically: he feels threatened by other big political figures. This is how Alter puts it:

> He wasn't comfortable with prominent figures who might not easily be managed by his White House. His cabinet did have Hillary Clinton, but not other camera-ready, large-than-life characters who might have taken some of the pressure off him had they been allowed to represent the administration more often.

As a result of this in his second term, Obama has tended to promote from within instead of reaching out for harder-to-control but better-qualified people to serve in his administration. New York mayor Michael Bloomberg would have been one such character when it came to the economy, business and investment, but he has never been asked.

This same love of personal privacy means that Obama probably takes too many decisions after receiving too little varied and competing advice. This became most obvious in the tangle which the President got himself into over Syria in the early autumn of 2013. In an off-the-cuff remark — itself a worrying trait — Obama had drawn his 'red line' about the use of nerve gas by the Syrian regime of Bashar al-Assad. After such illegal weapons were used by Assad in August, Obama then spent some two to three weeks arguing for a 'limited' use of American military force to stop, or at least possibly deter, the Assad regime from using them again. Then on 10 September, the President went on primetime television to summon up support for his policy. But Obama's speech was a shambles — long on rhetoric but short on resolve. The media, from the liberal *New York Times* to the conservative *Wall Street Journal*, panned the speech (see Box 7.1). Daniel Henninger in the *Wall Street Journal* christened the Obama White House 'the Laurel and Hardy presidency' mindful of Oliver Hardy's oft-repeated lament to his bumbling accomplice Stan Laurel: 'Here's another nice mess you've gotten us into.'

> ### Box 7.1 Media headlines following President Obama's 10 September television address to the nation on Syria
>
> - 'Amateur hour in the White House' (Maureen Dowd, *New York Times*)
> - 'The President embarrasses the nation' (John Podhoretz, *New York Post*)
> - 'An incoherent mess of a speech' (Nile Gardiner, *Daily Telegraph*)
> - 'Stumbling toward Damascus' (Joe Klein, *Time*)
> - 'What was the President thinking?' (Megan McArdle, *Bloomberg*)
> - 'Obama's debacle inflicts historic damage' (Peter Wehner, *Commentary*)
> - 'The Laurel and Hardy presidency' (Daniel Henninger, *Wall Street Journal*)

But how did the President make such a shambles of this? Where was the advice giving? One only has to read the extracts from the speech given in Box 7.2 to see that this was a classic example of the biblical adage, 'If the trumpet gives an uncertain sound, who will prepare for battle?'

Joe Klein in *Time* magazine called this 'one of the more stunning and inexplicable displays of presidential incompetence' that he could remember. But Klein's diagnosis was most interesting:

> The failure cuts straight to the heart of a perpetual criticism of the Obama White House: that the President thinks he can do policy-making all on his own. This has been the most closely-guarded American foreign policy-making process since President Richard Nixon and his National Security Adviser Henry Kissinger, only in this White House, there's no Kissinger.

Box 7.2 Extracts from President Obama's television address on Syria

- 'If we fail to act, the Assad regime will see no reason to stop using chemical weapons.'
- 'That is why after careful deliberation, I determined that it is in the national security interests of the United States to respond to the Assad regime's use of chemical weapons through a targeted strike.'
- 'Even though I possess the authority to order military strikes I believed it was right, in the absence of a direct or imminent threat to our security, to take this debate to Congress.'
- 'However, over the last few days, we've seen some encouraging signs [including] constructive talks I had with President Putin. The Russian government has indicated a willingness to join with the international community in pushing Assad to give up his chemical weapons.'
- 'I have therefore asked the leaders of Congress to postpone a vote to authorise the use of force while we pursue this diplomatic path.'

Obama has no Henry Kissinger (Nixon's foreign policy guru) or Brent Scowcroft (who played the same role for both Gerald Ford and the first George Bush), no one who can say to the president with some authority, 'Mr President, you're doing the wrong thing here. This policy is a nonsense.' And did no one raise with the President the question of why go to Congress at all for their approval for a *limited* strike? Sources in the administration suggested that his senior staff — many new to their jobs in the second term — did indeed raise this question, but Obama ignored them. This suggests another problem, namely that the staff are weak and ineffective.

Failure to control both houses of Congress

Second term presidents rarely enjoy their own party in the majority in either, let alone both, houses of Congress. As Table 7.5 shows, taking the 16 years of the second terms of Eisenhower, Reagan, Clinton and George W. Bush, the president's party controlled both houses for only 2 years (Bush's Republicans in 2005–06) and controlled one house for a further 2 years (Reagan's Republicans in the Senate in 1985–86).

Table 7.5 President's party control of House and Senate during second term

President	Dates	Control of House (years)	Control of Senate (years)
Dwight Eisenhower	1957–60	0/4	0/4
Ronald Reagan	1985–88	0/4	2/4
Bill Clinton	1997–2000	0/4	0/4
George W. Bush	2005–08	2/4	2/4
Totals		**2/16**	**4/16**

Obama's likely failure to control the House of Representatives throughout his second term will be a significant hindrance to his chances of legislative and policy success. As I write this chapter, the headline in today's *Washington Post* reads: 'SHUTDOWN BEGINS: 800,000 federal workers to be furloughed; parks, monuments and museums are closed.' The cause of this partial closure of the federal government was a failure of the Democrat-controlled Senate and the Republican-controlled House to reach an agreement on a temporary budget resolution which would have kept the federal government in money after the failure to agree a budget by the 1 October deadline. House Republicans wanted to tie any temporary budget deal to a 1-year delay in the funding of President Obama's healthcare legislation. The Senate Democrats — and the President — found this completely unacccptablc, hence gridlock. If only Obama hadn't lost those 63 House seats back in 2010 — the worst performance by the president's party in the first set of mid-term elections for 88 years.

Increased levels of partisanship

This final factor takes us back to the subject of Chapter 5 — partisanship. In previous eras, even if a president did not enjoy party control of both houses of Congress there was a good chance that he could still enact his policies by working with so-called 'moderates' or 'centrists' from the other party and thereby building a winning cross-party coalition. A Democrat president like Lyndon Johnson or Jimmy Carter could attract some moderate, northeastern Republicans; a Republican like Ronald Reagan or the first George Bush could attract some conservative, southern Democrats. But nowadays there are a number of problems with this scenario.

First, members of the opposing party don't want to be seen working with the president. It's the fastest way to be labelled a 'moderate' or a 'centrist' and thereby invite an intra-party challenge in the primary from a more conservative (in the case of a Republican) or more liberal (in the case of a Democrat) opponent. There is a long list of senators who have had this unhappy experience, and a number will face it in 2014 including Republicans Lamar Alexander of Tennessee, Lindsey Graham of South Carolina, and Mike Enzi of Wyoming. Enzi is being challenged by Liz Cheney, the elder daughter of the former vice-president Dick Cheney. In a recent interview with *National Journal,* Cheney criticised Senator Enzi for having 'negotiated for months as part of the Gang of Six for Obamacare in 2009'. The Gang of Six was a group of Democrats and Republicans in the Senate who tried to work together with the President on healthcare reform. 'That was a big mistake,' commented Cheney. 'He gave cover to President Obama. He should have opposed it from the very beginning.'

Second, partisanship is now so rife in Washington that as soon as the president — of whichever party — proposes some policy, the members of the other party will automatically oppose it. No matter, for example, that Obamacare looked a lot like the healthcare reform which Republican Mitt Romney introduced in Massachusctts when he was governor of the state. If it's Obama's policy, Republicans will oppose it. Indeed polling evidence exists to suggest that ordinary Americans could be in favour of a certain policy, but if they are then told it is 'President Obama's policy', Republicans will suddenly be opposed to it. And Democrats' reaction to President George W. Bush's policies was equally predictably negative.

Third, as we saw in Chapter 5, moderates and centrists in Congress have become an endangered species. There are hardly any of them left. So discussion about how a president can woo them is almost meaningless anyway.

Conclusions

The *Time* magazine cover for 9 September 2013, bore the headline: 'The Unhappy Warrior: Barack Obama ran for President to get the US out of wars, not into them.' Underneath this cover headline was a small picture of a diminutive and sad-looking President Obama. It reminded me of a cover of the same journal which appeared in June 1993 entitled in huge letters 'The Incredible Shrinking President' and underneath a tiny picture of President Bill Clinton. That said, the Clinton cover story proved to be wrong. Clinton didn't 'shrink' and served out what today is mostly regarded as a successful two-term administration, with one glaring exception.

Four things will, I think, be key in determining how Obama's second term turns out. First, how will the economy turn out? Much of Clinton's success — indeed at one point his very survival — can be attributed to a revitalised economy. If Obama presides over a similar economic resurgence, he will be forgiven much else. Second, how will foreign adventures and problems turn out — Iraq, Afghanistan, Egypt and Syria to name but four — and how will his relationships develop with key world leaders such as Putin of Russia and Merkel in Germany? Third, how will the Obamacare rollout develop? Will it continue to be an embarrassing series of mishaps? Fourth, how will his party fare in the 2014 mid-term elections? Ronald Reagan in 1986 and George W. Bush in 2006 both suffered severe reversals in their second term mid-terms. But in 1998 Clinton's Democrats actually won five seats in the House and came out evens in the Senate. Who will Obama imitate? There is still much to be decided in the legacy of President Barack Obama.

Questions

1 What kind of presidency did the Founding Fathers create?
2 How did Obama's re-election compare with that of previous second term presidents with regard to the Electoral College and the popular vote?
3 What evidence is there that second term presidents are less successful in Congress than first term presidents?
4 Analyse the data presented in Table 7.4.
5 What other problems do presidents often face in their second terms?
6 What does Jonathan Alter mean by saying that Obama 'doesn't much like the public parts of the presidency'?
7 What was wrong with Obama's television address on Syria in September 2013?
8 What do the data in Table 7.5 tell us about a president's likelihood of enjoying party control of Congress in his second term?
9 Why does Obama face such difficulties in trying to build cross-party support in Congress?

Chapter 8

The federal government shutdown, or a mad tea party?

Fact or fiction?

The seventh chapter in Lewis Carroll's *Alice's Adventures in Wonderland* is entitled 'A Mad Tea Party', popularly known as the Mad Hatter's Tea Party. Alice arrives to find a table set out under a tree with the March Hare, the Hatter, and the Dormouse seated at it.

> 'No room! No room!' they cried out when they saw Alice coming.

> 'There's *plenty* of room!' said Alice indignantly, and she sat down in a large armchair at one end of the table.

I was tempted to write this chapter as a skit on Carroll's story ...

> 'Have some concessions,' the President said in an encouraging tone.

> Senator Cruz looked all round the table, but there was nothing on it. 'I don't see any concessions,' he remarked.

> 'There aren't any,' said the President.

> 'Then it wasn't very civil of you to offer them,' said the Senator angrily.

> 'It wasn't very civil of you to sit down without being invited,' said the President.

> 'I didn't know it was *your* table,' said Senator Cruz.

> 'Your budget wants cutting,' said the House Speaker addressing the President.

> 'You shouldn't make personal remarks,' the President retorted with some severity, 'it's very rude.'

I could have gone on. For the story of last year's partial shutdown of the federal government ended up as a doleful story about America's Tea Party movement in general, and Texas senator Ted Cruz in particular. And there must surely have been some Democrats who fancied the role of the Queen of Hearts in the Carroll original — with her oft-repeated cry, 'Off with his head!'

Gridlock in Congress

On 1 October 2013, the non-essential parts of the United States federal government were temporarily shut down for what in the end was a period of 16 days after Congress failed to agree a budget for the fiscal year 2014.

This was the first federal government shutdown since the two that occurred in 1995–96 when Democrat president Bill Clinton failed to persuade Republican House speaker Newt Gingrich to pass the 1996 budget. With the 2014 budget stalled in Congress, a temporary budget — called a 'continuing appropriations resolution' — had to be passed by both houses to keep all parts of the government running from 1 October. But the Republican-controlled House and the Democrat-controlled Senate could not agree on the terms of the continuing resolution.

On 20 September, the House passed a continuing resolution by 230 votes to 189. But the Republican majority had written into the resolution a defunding of 'Obamacare' — President Obama's healthcare reform legislation — which Democrats in both chambers found totally unacceptable. The House vote was almost entirely along party lines with only one Republican (Scott Rigell of Virginia) voting 'no' and only two Democrats (Jim Matheson of Utah and Mike McIntyre of North Carolina) voting 'yes'. Keeping in mind what we discovered in Chapter 5 it is worth noting that Matheson and McIntyre are two of the nine so-called Romney Democrats — Democrat House members whose constituents voted for Republican Mitt Romney in 2012. Romney polled 68% in Matheson's Utah district, and 59% in McIntyre's North Carolina district.

Four days after the House vote, the Senate was treated to a filibuster — the *Washington Post* denied it was truly a filibuster and described it as merely a 'talkathon' — by Texas senator Ted Cruz, the poster boy of the Tea Party movement. The whatever-it-was lasted for 21 hours and 19 minutes which, as Table 8.1 shows, put him fourth in the filibuster league table and made this the longest Senate speech for almost 30 years.

Table 8.1 Senate filibusters of longer than 10 hours

Senator	Date begun	Measure	Length (hrs:mins)
Strom Thurmond	28 August 1957	Civil Rights Act	24:18
Alfonse D'Amato	17 October 1986	Defense Authorization Act	23:30
Wayne Morse	24 April 1953	Submerged Lands Act	22:26
Ted Cruz	**24 September 2013**	**Continuing Resolution**	**21:19**
Robert LaFollette	29 May 1908	Aldrich–Vreeland Act	18:23
William Proxmire	28 September 1981	Debt ceiling increase	16:12
Huey Long	12 June 1935	National Industrial Recovery Act	15:30
Alfonse D'Amato	5 October 1992	Revenue Act	15:14
Robert Byrd	9 June 1964	Civil Rights Act	14:13
Rand Paul	6 March 2013	Confirmation of CIA Director	12:52

Cruz used his talkathon to castigate Obamacare (see Box 8.1). Listening to Cruz is itself an interesting experience, for his use of exaggeration and overstatement is habitual. In the style of Senator Joe McCarthy of Communist witch-hunt fame, one almost expected the Texan to pull a piece of paper out of his pocket and claim: 'I have here in my hand a list of 205 names that have supported Obamacare and who nevertheless are still working and shaping policy in the Health and Human Services Department.' (In a speech in Wheeling, West Virginia, in February 1950, Senator McCarthy had claimed 'The State Department is infested with Communists. I have here in my hand a list of 205 — a list of names that were made known to the Secretary of State as being members of the Communist Party and who nevertheless are still working and shaping policy in the State Department.')

Cruz's speech was not all politics. Literary quotations were as varied as the children's storybook *The Little Engine That Could*, and the Old Testament book of *Proverbs*. There was even a bedtime story — *Green Ham and Eggs* — for the Senator's two young daughters watching on C-SPAN.

Box 8.1	Descriptions of Obamacare in Senator Cruz's speech

- 'a train wreck'
- 'not working'
- 'destroying jobs'
- 'driving up healthcare costs'
- 'killing health benefits'
- 'the biggest job killer in this country'
- 'destroying the 40-hour working week'
- 'destroying the backbone of the middle class'
- 'forcing more and more people into part-time employment'
- 'really, really, really bad'

Cruz's talkathon achieved little other than to waste time and make it even less likely that the House and Senate would be able to come up with an agreeable compromise before the 1 October deadline. The Senate passed a continuing resolution by 54 votes to 44, but this one *included* funding for Obamacare. All 54 'yes' votes were cast by Democrats and all 44 'no' votes were cast by Republicans. Two Republicans — Jeff Flake of Arizona and Orrin Hatch of Utah — did not vote. Back it went to the House, who reinstated the defunding of Obamacare. Back it went to the Senate who removed it again. The President and his congressional Democrats wouldn't compromise; neither would the Republicans. Indeed, some Republican members of Congress sounded rather like young British soldiers going off to fight in the Great War in 1914. Looking ahead to the imminent shutdown, Michelle Bachmann commented:

We're very excited. It's exactly what we wanted, and we got it. People will be very grateful … This is about the happiest I've seen [Republican] members [of Congress] in a long time, because we see we are starting to win this dialogue on a national level.

On 1 October large swathes of the federal government closed down and many civil servants were put on unpaid furlough.

Political manoeuvring

On the eve of the shutdown, President Obama called a cabinet meeting at the White House — the second meeting of the Obama cabinet in less than 3 weeks. One could not help thinking, however, that the meeting was more for the photo opportunity beforehand than any real usefulness in promoting government efficiency (see Box 8.2).

Box 8.2	President Obama's comments to the press before cabinet meeting, 30 September 2013

This is my Cabinet. And we're going to be discussing the impacts, potentially, of a shutdown and how all of these various agencies will be managing to make sure the core essential functions continue, but also, obviously, to help try to manage what's going to be a very difficult situation for the employees of all of these agencies, who are doing outstanding and very difficult work all across the country.

So I appreciate all the members of the Cabinet who are here. They have been doing a lot of planning. I wish they were spending more time focusing on how to grow jobs and the economy as opposed to having to spend time figuring out how they manage a government shutdown. But as always, they're prepared. And we'll be getting a full briefing from the entire crew during the course of this meeting.

Source: www.whitehouse.gov

For much of the first week of the shutdown, both sides held their ground. Tea Party Republicans lobbied House Speaker John Boehner not to allow any compromise bill on to the House floor which did not include the defunding of Obamacare. Democrats, meanwhile, took to the airwaves with equally exaggerated language to denounce the congressional Republicans for their tactics.

By week two there were signs of change. Not only was there now a budget to agree, but also Congress was nearer another deadline — that to raise the government's debt ceiling to avoid the United States defaulting on the public debt. Treasury Secretary Jacob Lew had warned that default would become a reality if the debt ceiling was not raised by 17 October. And so the political manoeuvring began as this second deadline loomed.

Box 8.3	Presidential meetings on government shutdown and debt ceiling, 8–15 October 2013
Tuesday 8	President delivers statement and answers questions from the press
Wednesday 9	President conducts regional television interviews President and vice-president meet with House Democratic caucus
Thursday 10	President and vice-president meet with Senate Democratic caucus President and vice-president meet with House Republican leadership
Friday 11	President and vice-president meet with Senate Republican caucus
Tuesday 15	President conducts television interviews President meets with members of House Democratic leadership

Box 8.3 shows the meetings that the President held during the next 7 days as Congress moved slowly and painfully towards a resolution of the crisis. By the time the President had met with the House Republican leadership on Thursday 10th, the Republican leader in the Senate, Mitch McConnell, was admitting that the Republicans had backed the wrong horse and committed a serious political gaffe in provoking the shutdown. McConnell now turned his back on the Tea Party tribe and turned instead to more conciliatory Senate Republicans such as Lamar Alexander and Susan Collins who were already talking with Democrats. By the following Monday, the Senate majority and minority leaders had reached a deal.

Meanwhile in the House, Speaker John Boehner had completely lost control of his Republican caucus. He put two proposed continuing resolutions to them, but they rejected both. Thus with the House stymied, the focus was on the Senate to lead the way. On Wednesday 16th, with just hours to go to the debt ceiling deadline, the Senate passed a continuing resolution — that included Obamacare funding — by 81 votes to 18. Twenty-seven Republicans joined all 54 Democrats to pass it, with 18 Republicans voting 'no'. Many House Republicans accused their Senate colleagues of betrayal, but the game was up. 'We fought the good fight, but we just didn't win,' admitted Speaker Boehner. The Senate bill passed the House by 285 votes to 144 with the Democratic caucus united (all 198 voting in favour) and the Republicans hopelessly divided — 87 voting 'yes' and 144 voting 'no'. Recriminations abounded as the President signed the bill into law just after midnight.

Winners and losers

That's the easy part — Obama and the Democrats won; the Speaker, Ted Cruz, the Tea Party and the Republican Party lost, big time. It was a humiliation (see Box 8.4). Just a week later, the *Washington Post*/ABC News poll found that the Republican Party's unfavourability ratings were at an all-time high of 63%. They were up 10 percentage points among women, 17 points among independents, and 19 points among seniors, all of whom will be key voting blocs in the 2014 mid-term elections.

<table>
<tr><td>Box 8.4</td><td>'The Republican Surrender', New York Times, 16 October 2013</td></tr>
</table>

The Republican Party slunk away on Wednesday from its failed, ruinous strategy to get its way through the use of havoc. Hours away from an inevitable [stock] market crash, it approved a deal that could have been achieved months ago had a few more lawmakers set aside their animosity. After President Obama signs the bill, the government will reopen after more than two weeks of shutdown, and the threat of a default will be lifted. The health care reform law will not be defunded or delayed. No taxes will be cut, and the deal calls for no new cuts to federal spending or limits to social welfare programs. The only thing Republicans achieved were billions of dollars in damage to the economy, harm to the nation's reputation and a rock-bottom public approval rating.

Within a few days, even the granddaddy of American conservative magazines the *National Review* was saying that as far as the antics of the congressional Tea Partiers were concerned, it was a case of 'enough already', describing their ideology as 'mistaken'. All the Republicans can hope is that voters have short memories. They must also hope that voters will focus on other issues which may make them less kindly disposed to the Democrats: continued sloppiness in the rollout of Obamacare; a weak economy; and an incumbent president with a typical end of second term approval rating.

But the President is not without blame. As Dan Balz concluded in his most recent book on Obama (*Collision 2012*, Penguin Group, 2013):

> Presidents are expected to solve problems and overcome political obstacles. Did Obama ever have a strategy to achieve that goal? Should he — could he — have built better relationships with congressional Republicans?

This takes us back to Obama's personal weaknesses that we discussed in Chapter 7. Republicans also remembered that during the debt ceiling crisis of 2006, the then junior senator from Illinois stated during the Senate debate 'The fact that we are here today to debate raising America's debt limit is a sign of leadership failure.' That senator then went on to announce that 'I therefore intend to oppose the effort to increase America's debt limit.' That senator was Barack Obama. And he accused Mitt Romney throughout the 2012 election campaign of flip-flopping on issues? On the debt ceiling, the President is a major league flip-flopper.

However, what is of greater concern is what these 16 days said about the current state of American politics. The underlying theme of so much we have covered in this year's *Update* is increased polarisation, partisanship and gridlock. The American Constitution was an invitation to do deals. It was based, in the words of one sage commentator, on 'three fundamental principles — compromise, compromise and compromise'. With compromise now a dirty word, we fear for the future of productive, workable government in Washington during the coming years. Maybe this experience will embolden the Republican leadership to face down the Tea Partiers. If not, we're likely to be in for more episodes of *Washington's Adventures in Wonderland*.

Questions

1 Why did the partial government shutdown occur on 1 October 2013?
2 What did Senator Cruz's filibuster achieve?
3 Assess the role of the Tea Party movement in these events.
4 Why do you think the Republican leader in the Senate Mitch McConnell concluded that his party had made 'a serious political gaffe' in provoking the shutdown?
5 Why was President Obama open to criticism over these events?
6 How does this event illustrate the heightened levels of partisanship in Washington?

Who's Who in US politics 2014

Bold = second term appointees

Executive branch

President	Barack Obama
Vice President	Joe Biden

The Cabinet

Secretary of State	**John Kerry**
Secretary of Defense	**Chuck Hagel**
Secretary of the Treasury	**Jacob Lew**
Secretary of Agriculture	Tom Vilsack
Secretary of the Interior	**Sally Jewell**
Attorney General (Justice Department)	Eric Holder
Secretary of Commerce	**Penny Pritzker**
Secretary of Labor	**Thomas Perez**
Secretary of Health and Human Services	Kathleen Sebelius
Secretary of Education	Arne Duncan
Secretary of Housing and Urban Development	Shaun Donovan
Secretary of Transportation	**Anthony Foxx**
Secretary of Energy	**Ernest Moniz**
Secretary of Veterans' Affairs	Eric Shinseki
Secretary of Homeland Security	Janet Napolitano

Executive Office of the President personnel

White House Chief of Staff	**Denis McDonough**
Director of Office of Management and Budget	**Sylvia Mathews Burwell**
Chairman of Council of Economic Advisers	**Jason Furman**
Domestic Policy Council Director	Cecilia Munoz
National Security Adviser	**Susan Rice**
Assistant to the President for Legislative Affairs	**Miguel Rodriguez**
Trade Representative	**Michael Froman**
Press Secretary	Jay Carney

Legislative branch

Senate leadership

President *Pro Tempore* of the Senate   Patrick Leahy (D-Vermont)
Senate Majority Leader   Harry Reid (D-Nevada)
Senate Minority Leader   Mitch McConnell (R-Kentucky)
Senate Majority Whip   Richard Durbin (D-Illinois)
Senate Minority Whip   John Cornyn (R-Texas)

Senate Standing Committee chairs

Agriculture, Nutrition and Forestry	Debbie Stabenow	Michigan
Appropriations	Barbara Mikulski	Maryland
Armed Services	Carl Levin	Michigan
Banking, Housing and Urban Affairs	Tim Johnson	South Dakota
Budget	Patty Murray	Washington
Commerce, Science and Transportation	Jay Rockefeller	West Virginia
Energy and Natural Resources	Ron Wyden	Oregon
Environment and Public Works	Barbara Boxer	California
Finance	Max Baucus	Montana
Foreign Relations	Robert Menendez	New Jersey
Health, Education, Labor and Pensions	Tom Harkin	Iowa
Homeland Security and Governmental Affairs	Tom Carper	Delaware
Judiciary	Patrick Leahy	Vermont
Rules and Administration	Charles Schumer	New York
Small Business and Entrepreneurship	Mary Landrieu	Louisiana
Veterans' Affairs	Bernie Sanders	Vermont

House leadership

Speaker of the House of Representatives   John Boehner (R-Ohio)
House Majority Leader   Eric Cantor (R-Virginia)
House Minority Leader   Nancy Pelosi (D-California)
House Majority Whip   Kevin McCarthy (R-California)
House Minority Whip   Steny Hoyer (D-Maryland)

House Standing Committee chairs

Agriculture	Frank Lucas	Oklahoma
Appropriations	Harold Rogers	Kentucky
Armed Services	Howard 'Buck' McKeon	California
Budget	Paul Ryan	Wisconsin
Education and the Workforce	John Kline	Minnesota
Energy and Commerce	Fred Upton	Michigan
Financial Services	Jeb Hensarling	Texas
Foreign Affairs	Ed Royce	California
Homeland Security	Mike McCaul	Texas
Judiciary	Bob Goodlatte	Virginia
Natural Resources	Doc Hastings	Washington
Oversight and Government Reform	Darrell Issa	California
Rules	Pete Sessions	Texas
Science, Space and Technology	Lamar Smith	Texas
Small Business	Sam Graves	Missouri
Transportation and Infrastructure	Bill Shuster	Pennsylvania
Veterans' Affairs	Jeff Miller	Florida
Ways and Means	Dave Camp	Michigan

Judicial branch

		Appointed by	Year
Chief Justice	John Roberts	George W. Bush	2005
Associate Justices	Antonin Scalia	Ronald Reagan	1986
	Anthony Kennedy	Ronald Reagan	1988
	Clarence Thomas	George H. W. Bush	1991
	Ruth Bader Ginsburg	Bill Clinton	1993
	Stephen Breyer	Bill Clinton	1994
	Samuel Alito	George W. Bush	2006
	Sonia Sotomayor	Barack Obama	2009
	Elena Kagan	Barack Obama	2010